" When an antique dealer friend visited from California, he was impressed with the quality of trash I was finding and wanted to try his hand. I had him write a list of the items he wanted and then we set off to wander the streets at random, watching for the items to materialize in the trash piles.

" After roving several neighborhoods, I found the things I wanted, but my friend found nothing that interested him. He insisted I had some special power that he lacked. I assured him this wasn't true, but that I did make certain assumptions that most "normal" people didn't. I fully believed that

1) anything is possible;

2) I deserved to have what I wanted and,

3) that it wasn't necessary to work hard
    in order to get what I wanted

"Most people believe what our society teaches — that we are limited by our physical reality (some things are possible and others aren't), that you must do something to be deserving, and that you must earn what you get. Somehow, I never fully bought these fundamental beliefs of our culture.

"After speaking of these principles to my friend, he sheepishly admitted that what he put on his list were only the items he thought might be possible to find in the trash. He hadn't listed the things he **really** wanted, because he considered them too valuable for someone to throw out. I suggested he make a new list and that we go hunting again the next morning . . ."

from **Living Inside Out**

Living Inside Out

Saying Yes to the Inner Voice

Living Inside Out

Saying Yes to the Inner Voice

Ellen Fritz Solart

Desert Sage Publishing Mayer, Arizona

Published by Desert Sage Publishing
HC 60, Box 4135
Mayer, AZ 86333

Cover art by Frank Boros
Electronic layout by Paul Bagley

Printed in the United States of America
Library of Congress Catalog Card Number: 98-94794

ISBN 0-9663043-1-4

For Youri and Allen

Acknowledgments

I have always read the long lists of acknowledgments in books with interest. Now I know why the lists are so long. Putting a book out is a co-creative process. Without the many cheerleaders, supporters and helpers, it would be a much more difficult task and a very lonely one. I am very grateful that the right person has always come along at the right time.

Jessica Lipnack was the first person to see my manuscript in its early stages and was the spark plug that ignited my fire. **Derenna Muckjian** blessed me when she unknowingly validated the very reason I have written this book. She called me, bewildered, saying something deep inside her was changing because she was reading the manuscript. **Michael Sayre** inspired me to loosen up and fly right! He helped set my tone with his early editings.

Next came a series of cheerleaders, the most consistent being my cousin, **Nancy Holtshouse.** Many others have encouraged, proofed and commented—

THANK YOU ALL! Special thanks to **Ed Mickens** and **Frank Boros** for their friendship, gentle prodding and professional expertise. Like model parents, **Mike White**, my publishing coach, and **Tama White**, my editor, have waited patiently in the background giving me solid support as I needed it and a constant loving presence, both crucial to my success.

Note to the Reader

Although this book is about me, it is also about you. I see the process of my spiritual awakening as the classic steps we all go through as we open up to our innate knowing. The actual story, the details, are different for each one of us, but the essence is the same.

As we experience life, there are clues that lead us through the fog we are conditioned to accept as reality. We can choose to ignore the clues and continue to be knocked around by outside "circumstances," or we can learn to pay attention and be empowered by our inner authority. It is a matter of choice. No matter who you are, or what your life environment, there is always an individualized trail that leads to freedom and personal fulfillment. I have written this book with hopes of nurturing your spiritual process no matter where along this path you are.

To benefit the most, I suggest you read from front to back—without skimming through to get the gist or peeking at the ending. This is a book meant for the intuitive mind, with sequential triggers for the subconscious while the rational mind follows the story.

Thanks for reading. . . and listening.

Contents

Knowing

This was different from my other knowings. This one left me stunned. The mere mention of Philadelphia by my dorm mate had precipitated a physical response so strong I nearly passed out in my chair. It was as if someone had punched me in the stomach and knocked me in the head at the same time. My head swirled as I felt myself drawing inward, whirlpooling into the center of my being so quickly I lost all awareness of the room and its occupants. Then abruptly the sensations stopped and suddenly I knew: Philadelphia was where I would go.

Dazed, I slowly realized the travelogue had ended. I could hear the voices of the other girls around me as they strolled out of the lounge. My roommate stood up and smiled down at me, waiting. I rose obediently from my chair and followed after her down the hall in my trance-like state.

By the time we reached our room I was feeling more myself. I asked my roommate if she had a map of the United States. She shook her head and scowled curiously at me. I didn't take the time to explain. Instead I dashed out the door to the next room, my roommate following close behind. When I was handed an atlas, I anxiously flipped the pages looking for Pennsylvania. "I'm going to Philadelphia after graduation," I announced to the three friends now gawking at me.

"For God's sake, why?" one of them asked.

Really I had no idea why I was going to Philadelphia. For years I dreamed about living a simple life in the Australian outback and writing for some magazine there. It was what I thought I wanted. I hadn't considered any other options.

With my finger firmly marking the Philadelphia dot on the map, I looked up and replied in my best rational tone, "Philadelphia is out east, near the ocean—sort of—and near New York, but not New York."

A knowing look passed between my three friends, and I could tell they thought this was just another of my irrational ideas. As usual, they didn't take me seriously. Graduation from the University of Wisconsin was over two years away; much could happen before then.

For days the sudden Philadelphia realization consumed me. I couldn't think of anything else. Although my life in a Big Eastern City would be very different than my imagined Australian one, my dream to write for a magazine remained constant. Now, however, I recognized with every fiber of my being that the magazine I would write for was no where else but in Philadelphia. This startling fact of my knowing gave my life new direction and, somehow, new stability. It began to be a concrete base I could build my plans on.

Never before had a knowing been so substantial or had such an effect on me. In fact, I never even used the term "knowing" for this kind of experience. Sometimes I just noticed in retrospect that something I had strong feelings about proved to be true. At other times, information just came to me when I needed it, out of the blue, when I knew the answer to a question but had no idea *how* I knew.

Of all my knowings prior to this, there was only one I consciously recognized. I was at home lying on the couch reading the last chapter of *Gone With The Wind* for a high school book report. When I read those last emotional lines, my heart ached and tears streamed down my cheeks. I closed the book and closed my eyes, savoring the moment. Strangely, the image of a little girl suddenly appeared to me. She reached toward me calling, "Auntie Ellen, Auntie Ellen!" Startled, I opened my eyes and wondered for a moment. As yet I didn't have any nieces, but the oldest of my three sisters was pregnant. Then it came to me.

"Carol is going to have a girl!" I exclaimed to my parents sitting close by. My mom and dad glanced up from reading the newspaper, smiled and said, "Oh really? That would be nice." When my brother-in-law called several months later to announce the birth of his first daughter, no one remembered my prediction except me. It didn't matter. What did matter was that it made me notice something different had happened inside me.

Although my dorm friends had witnessed the outcome of my knowings before, they didn't recognize them as anything precise. They saw them as sort of "conclusions" I came to without thinking. When I announced I would be going to Philadelphia and didn't have a clue where it was except in Pennsylvania somewhere, my friends had a good laugh and started kidding me about it. When, however, decisions I made based on my illogical "conclusions" worked out well for me (and usually they did), my friends were perplexed, to say the least. It had to be luck, dumb luck, they said. "It isn't fair," they insisted. "Why do you have so much luck and why aren't we as lucky?"

Several months after my Philadelphia knowing my three friends and I were talking about how much we wanted to go to the annual Military Ball. Suddenly, I announced offhandedly, "I'm going to go!"

"Who would invite *you* to the dance?" my friends mocked.

"I don't know," I admitted, "but I'm going!"

I wasn't dating anyone in particular and didn't know anyone in particular who might ask me. Still, I just suddenly *knew* I was going. It wasn't even positive thinking. In fact, this wasn't thinking at all. When

I had the notion about going, something inside me just clicked and I felt impelled to act. The next day I bought fabric and began sewing a dress.

When my dorm mates discovered what I was doing, they couldn't believe it and ridiculed me mercilessly. I retreated to some serene and good-natured place inside myself and told them with a smile, " Just wait and see, but I am going." My smile covered up the hurt feelings about being made fun of again.

The dance loomed closer, but I still didn't have a date. My friends made a "DATE WANTED" sign in my name and posted it on the cafeteria bulletin board. This quickly made me the laughing stock of the whole dorm complex. Though the ridicule embarrassed me, I felt no doubts about going to the dance. Past experience had taught me that sticking to my guns about what I knew to be true, even if I was laughed at, had its rewards. I kept my smile and worked on the dress even when the dance was less than a week away and I was still dateless.

Finally, two days before the dance, the phone rang. My roommate answered and called out, "It's for you. It's a man!" My three friends, hoping against hope, flocked around me as I took the receiver. It was a friend of mine from the men's dorm next door. He had a buddy coming from out of town who needed a date for the Military Ball. He wanted to know if I would go. I looked into the three pairs of eyes all fixed on me and replied in the sweetest, most enthusiastic voice I could muster, "Why, thank you, I'd love to go!" To see three mouths drop wide open, speechless, was a saccharine gratification I savored for weeks. Saturday night came and Cinderella went to the ball, after all. Left at home were all her doubting stepsisters, chagrined and wondering, "Is this more of Ellen's dumb luck, or what?"

During the two years following my Philadelphia knowing, it was the only option I considered seriously. Waiting for it to happen, however, was a longer, harder test of faith than any I had endured before. Graduation came and went. My friends found jobs in their fields while I still waited for my knowing to come true. This time, at least, the few jokes that were made were good-hearted and affectionate. My friends had witnessed my "luck" for four years and they had developed, though reluctantly, a sense of awe about it. In fact, sometimes they even bragged, "If Ellen says its going to happen, then it will!"

My exasperated advisor, waiting for her only graduate in home economics-journalism to fly the coop, and my father, hoping his hard-earned tuition money wouldn't go to waste, urged me to accept a local job. I would make a great reporter, my advisor insisted when I received an offer from Madison's *State Journal*. She could not understand why I was so apparently fixated on Philadelphia. Feebly I told her, "I want to get out of Wisconsin and see the world." There was no way to explain the real reason. She would never understand I just knew I had to be there.

With my advisor's help, I wrote letters to all the magazines we could find that had editorial offices in Philadelphia. Then, not knowing what else to do, I agreed to share an apartment with a friend, took two part-time jobs, and waited for something to turn up.

It was almost Christmas. Six long months of waiting had passed by the time my advisor received a call from the women's editor of the *Farm Journal*, a large national farm magazine based in Philadelphia. They needed an editorial assistant for the women's part of the journal, *The Farmer's Wife*. Even though I wasn't a farm girl, they were interested and said they wanted to talk with me.

My advisor gave them my number at the university limnology lab where I worked.

I was sitting at my desk when I received the call. An associate editor would be coming to Madison on assignment in a few days and she wanted to meet with me. When I put the receiver down I could hardly contain myself. I went running to find my supervisor.

"This is it!" I exclaimed, jumping up and down and hugging her. I knew without a doubt I would get the job.

"Let's go tell Professor Foster," she insisted.

Professor Foster was our good-looking and distinguished boss. Although he was in his fifties and I was just twenty-one, all the graduate students in the lab suspected we were having an affair. We didn't hide the fact that after work we often had lively and lengthy conversations and in general liked to kid each other. The truth was that Professor Foster was a good Mormon. Indeed, he was courting me—but not for himself. He wanted me to marry one of his four sons! When he heard my news, he was truly happy for me.

The associate editor was very casual in our meeting, but I sensed her astutely appraising me. When we parted she said I would be hearing from Philadelphia soon. Several days later I received another call from the *Farm Journal*. This time they wanted me to fly to Chicago to meet the women's editor herself.

I agreed and quickly made plane reservations. When I informed Professor Foster about my plans, he laughed. "What a coincidence," he said. "I'm flying the same day and about the same time for a meeting in Cincinnati! We have a reputation to live up to. Why don't you ride with me to the airport?" he offered with a grin.

A week later there were many raised eyebrows as we left the office together, arm in arm. The rumors that followed got even more juicy than before, and my supervisor, who appreciated a good joke, didn't spoil the game with the truth.

I met the women's editor, Miss Dieken, at the international restaurant at Chicago's O'Hare airport. I wore the new suit I bought especially for the occasion and hoped I appeared sophisticated and confident, although I felt neither.

Miss Dieken was pleasant and asked simple questions, but I had the impression she was,

Knowing

underneath, a shrewd and calculating woman. The
way she looked at me with her penetrating eyes as
she digested my every answer made me feel there was
more behind what she was asking than she let on. I
liked the challenge—guessing what she was really
after. I sensed she wanted me to be worldly enough
for the editorial staff of this large, national magazine
and yet folksy enough to relate to the readers.

I tried to appear worldly as I nonchalantly ate
the turtle soup I had ordered. I made sure to mention
all the childhood visits to my relatives' farms and the
semester I spent grooming a sheep for a university
livestock show, winning third prize. When all this
seemed to favorably impress Miss Dieken, I hoped
she would tell me right then the job was mine.
But she didn't.

She left and I went home and waited and waited,
but no word. Finally, I received an envelope with the
Farm Journal return address logo on it. I ripped it open,
so sure it was a job offer. It wasn't. It was a draft of a
manuscript and a note. I was to edit the copy and
return it as soon as possible. I did it and waited once
again.

It was a week before Christmas when at last Miss
Dieken called. She informed me that the job I had
known about and not-so-patiently waited for was
now really mine. I was to go to Philadelphia immediately after the holidays to begin my first week's training! What had struck me so deeply so long ago had
finally come true.

That evening, feeling enormously relieved and tremendously excited, I walked down the streets of Madison never feeling the pavement. On University Avenue the large black man with snowy white hair, who always before appeared completely preoccupied with his ritual window washing, stopped to watch me pass by. With twinkling eyes and a face that was one huge smile, he exclaimed, "Boy, is she happy!"

A few steps later, a stranger walked up along side of me slipping his arm through mine. Grinning, he said, "You know you are positively glowing! Would you come home and light up my Christmas tree?"

After he walked on, I thought to myself, I *do* feel wonderful, yes!

Landing the job in Philadelphia was enough in itself to make me elated. Then, in addition, my trust in my knowing had been validated. Recognizing this, something deep within me quickened. I could feel that whatever lay ahead was going to be extraordinary.

A New Me

Arriving in Center City Philadelphia after living in the Midwest all my life was like landing in a foreign country. The historic buildings reminded me more of Europe than of the America I knew. The customs and the way people spoke took some getting used to. It was embarrassing to keep asking people to repeat themselves as if they didn't speak English, but their accent and meanings for some words were unfamiliar to me. Alien as everything seemed, I loved the excitement and stimulation of having a new place to explore. I was relieved to discover that Philadelphia was not the cold, unwelcoming city I had been warned about. For me, it was the contrary. Cab drivers, sales people, the *Farm Journal* staff, and everyone I met, seemed eager to help and please me. Policemen called me "dear" as they ushered me across the street. Strangers offered to carry my heavy packages, or cheerfully steered me back on course when I lost my way.

But it wasn't the reception I received in Philadelphia that made the first three months in my new home city the hardest I had ever spent in my life. It was the adjustment going on *within* me. Although I had originally rejoiced at the prospect of going to a place where I didn't know anyone, now I felt lost and awkward because of it. But it would be worth the suffering if, in this new environment that had no resemblance or ties to my life in Wisconsin, I could develop new aspects of myself. I hoped I could drop the "nut" image I hid behind and express my whole self without holding back.

My inside self was continually evolving, but I found it difficult to reflect these changes outwardly with people who knew me well. Whenever I said or did anything that didn't fit the image of good ol' Ellen, I was laughed at or asked if anything was wrong—perhaps I was sick? Those times made me feel guilty about being someone other than the person I was assumed to be. Set patterns could be harder to change than to perpetuate. Instead of risking rejection, I continued to play out the role most familiar. Consequently, my behaviors became habits rather than expressing my up-dated self.

Even as far back as high school, expressing my whole, or true self, had been my goal and also my challenge. I found it helped to have a strategy. When I evaluated how I could express my true self and still be both accepted by my peers and approved of by my teachers, I determined that the first step was to fortify my reputation as a good student. For the beginning six weeks of each new school year I arrived at school punctually, was attentive in class, and handed my homework in on time. It was in those early crucial weeks that teachers formed their opinions of who were the "good students" and who were the "troublemakers." Once this was settled, I could relax. For the rest of the year, the teachers focused on shaping up the troublemakers and left the rest of us alone. I could then venture to creatively express more of myself with my classmates without suffering dire consequences. No one would suspect a good student of playing pranks or being disruptive.

Although it was my nature to be honest, responsible and studious, it was also my nature to be fun-loving, inventive, and even mischievous. This side of my personality could not find creative expression in a stifling school structure. Although I participated in as many extra-curricular activities as I had time for, and yelled my head off at school fooball games, I needed more. My suppressed creativity would emerge through imaginative schemes and impulsive pranks. I sprayed smelly perfume via a squirt gun at Youth Center dances, threw my classmate's shoe out a fourth floor window, narrowly missing the assistant principal, and carried out ingenious strategies to get out of classes legitimately. All this I accomplished without being suspected of wrongdoing. My reputation as a good student held firm. Even when I was brave enough to own up to a few of my pranks, no one took my confessions seriously. Who was I trying to cover up for, some renowned troublemaker I felt sorry for? The transgressions just didn't fit my image.

Being seen as an impeccable student had its advantages. It also had undesirable implications, like I was "Miss Moral Maturity." This suggestion set me apart from my peers in ways I didn't like. Even my closest friends, who I believed should know better, wouldn't discuss certain things, like sex, in front of me, or they apologized for swearing when I was around. I really wanted to be accepted as one of them and at the same time express my individuality. Trying to correct this misjudgment, I showed up one night at a popular bar that illegally served alcohol to high school students. In pure horror, one of my classmates clapped her hand over her mouth when she saw me and gasped, "Oh, no! Now even the honor students are coming here!" In another attempt to correct my purity image, I pushed to earn a detention by repeatedly arriving late to school. To my dismay, however, I was excused each time, no questions asked! "You must have a good reason, Ellen," they told me. I argued, then begged for a detention. When finally I succeeded and my fellow students saw me sitting with them at the detention table after school, they couldn't believe their eyes. "Ellen, what are *you* doing here?"

Gradually, with considerable effort, I managed to shape an image of myself with my friends that allowed more of the self I wanted to emerge. I earned the reputation as "nut." My troublemaker antics were viewed then as the idiosyncrasies of "good ol' Ellen" and not taken seriously. I could have my crazy moments, as long as most of the time I acted reasonably and responsibly.

Using my nut image as a cover, I ventured to express a deeper part of myself. I talked more openly about a reality I perceived beyond the obvious everyday one.

When I was alone in my bedroom at night listening to classical music, I would close my eyes and allow myself to link with a presence I felt, a sort of guardian spirit. Was this God? I wondered. I experienced a communion with everything that existed and felt an assurance that no matter what happened in my life, somehow I would always be all right. Then I opened to the silence, and listened for the answers to my questions: What is the universe? What is life? Sometimes, in straining to hear, I experienced a sensation of lifting outside myself—out, out, to where I blended with the emptiness of space. The immensity, the endlessness of infinity would overwhelm me. Quickly I opened my eyes, abruptly bringing myself back to the familiar reality of my room.

No matter how hard I tried to block out my questions, they persisted. What is the purpose of life? Why are we here? I began discussing these questions with my friends—often at parties in dark basements illuminated with red lights, situations where our peers would be off in the corners necking with their dates. There *had* to be some important reason for the existence of our world, I thought. Otherwise, why would there be such an enormous effort for us all to be here?

Inspired by my Sunday school teacher at the Congregational church my family belonged to, I turned to religion as a way to find the answers to these questions preoccupying my thoughts. When our class visited the services of many different religious denominations, I discovered Judaism. Something in the music and the ritual touched me deeply. I began attending Sabbath school with a Jewish friend. I also went to Mass occasionally with my Catholic friends, and visited a service at the Christian Science church with my mother.

No one had answers that satisfied me. My inquiry continued via essays I wrote for creative writing class and the nightly talks I had with Mother as we walked the dog. When I asked her about life, why we were here on earth, she told me her theory—that we are here to make the world a better place for the next people. This only brought up another question: then why are the next people here?

The more I searched, the more unanswered questions I had, and the more frustrated I became. The Bible offered some comfort, but there were too many things in it I didn't comprehend. I was seeking definition and solid validation for the inner reality I was experiencing. Unable to integrate my deeper experience with my outer expression, I prayed nightly for a solution. "Please God, make the outer me the same as the inner."

My experiments for expanding my self-expression continued my freshman year at the University of Wisconsin. At the large multi-faceted campus I had various circles of friends. With each, I experimented with different aspects of myself—outrageous and fun, coy and womanly, serious and philosophical—to see which self I liked the best and which self received the best response from my peers. For a while, this schizophrenia served me well, but keeping it up was another story. Sometimes when the different circles of friends mixed, I forgot which self I was supposed to be and said or did something outlandish with the wrong friends. Usually the reaction was dirty looks or silence, reminders I couldn't comfortably relax and be my whole self all the time, not if I wanted to be accepted.

I longed for one group of friends with whom I could be all my me's at once. Since this didn't happen, I hid. I stayed behind my nut image, the role I could feel most comfortable in. I even publicly defined myself as a "nut" in a three-minute introductory speech I gave to my freshman speech class. Smiling and swallowing my pride, I stood in front of the class and cheerfully admitted, "I am a nut." Then, while I watched our tall Texan professor sitting in the back of the room giving time cues, I gave several examples to prove this preposterous claim. When I reached the end of my speech, I still had one minute left. Suddenly, I scrunched my mouth into a fish face and flapped my hands along side of my cheeks for fins. Caught totally off guard, "Texas" fell off his chair roaring with laughter. By the time he regained his seat and checked his watch, my three minutes were up. I got an "A" for the speech. However, from then on I couldn't stand in front of the class without everyone laughing. In or out of class, I was rarely taken seriously. Of course, this was the effect I usually wanted, yet being laughed at when I wanted to be taken seriously made me feel misunderstood and lonely. This was a side-effect of my nut image I didn't want.

My questions about the universe and the why's of existence continued to preoccupy me. I wanted to talk to someone, but who? I attended several campus churches and their discussion groups. Still no answers. I began to wonder if I was the only one who was questioning the value of life as it appeared. "Don't be so serious, relax and enjoy life," I was told. I did enjoy it to a large extent, but I couldn't relax. A restlessness gnawed inside me. I longed to connect to someone or something with the deepest part of myself. Anytime I tried to engage my dorm friends in serious discussion, they laughed at me and I became the entertainment for the evening. Having sold them on my being a nut, I didn't blame them for not accepting my seriousness, but it made me all the more lonely and sad. I spent more time by myself, turning my search into my study of literature and philosophy. But the answers, it seemed, had to come from within myself, not from any outside source.

Gradually, I began accepting the fact that a part of me would always remain unsatisfied. The answers to my questions were not going to be forthcoming. I stopped initiating serious discussions and gave in to enjoying my friends in whatever ways I could.

Then one day, late in my freshman year, something happened that totally changed me, something that substantiated the reality I had been trying so hard to have defined and validated. While sitting under a tree studying, I paused to glance at my watch. Suddenly, without warning, I felt a "lifting" sensation. Up, up, up I went—very quickly, guided by a firm but gentle presence—out farther than I had ever gone before. When I stopped, I was in outer space looking back at earth. A wonderous presence engulfed me. I heard a booming voice say, "Ellen, do not be afraid. You have been feeling lonely and separated from other people for a reason." Then instantly I was imbued with understanding. I was "shown" the past, present and future of life on Earth. The evolution of humanity and my life's purpose within it became clear to me. I understood, then, that the role I would play in life would put me on the outside looking in, separate from other people in order to act as a beacon for others to follow. Then, just as suddenly as I had left, I was back under the tree again staring at my watch. I felt I had been gone for hours. Yet, no time had passed! I felt totally energized and renewed.

I grabbed my books and rushed back to the dorm. Excited, I told my friends what happened. For a brief moment they took me seriously. Then all the jokes began, and once again I was the source for entertainment. My nut image had totally backfired, like it did for the little child who cried wolf too often. Sadly, I left to be alone. Sitting in the quiet of my room, I pondered the significance of what had happened.

A heaviness was gone. I felt completely validated for the first time. Life *did* have a purpose. *I* had a purpose! My mind reeled, unable to comprehend all the implications of my experience. Whatever it was, a knowing came from it that served as a reference point for me from then on; I wasn't crazy—a reality other than the most obvious did exist and somehow it operated outside of time.

Not only did something inside me change, but my life changed, also. Finally, I could relax. I knew now that if I needed to know something about the nature of the world, the knowledge would come to me—I didn't have to search. I had only to live and be open. Finally, too, I had found someone to talk to.

Peggy lived off campus, but she often came to eat dinner in our cafeteria. I found her to be a perfect mirror for me. She was another "nut" questioning the why of life, trying to find a more adequate way to express her true self. We became the Bobsey Twins, inseparable. People commented on how alike we were—our actions, our thoughts, the pitch of our voices, the way we laughed. Although we didn't resemble each other physically (I was short and light-haired, she was taller and dark-haired), we often wore clothes that had similar styles and were the same colors. Once, when we met for Sunday dinner, we arrived wearing identical outfits! We would never have planned it; we were too individual.

At last I had someone to explore the world with. Peggy understood what I said, what I felt. She had the right combination of seriousness and "creativity." We spent hours discussing our innermost thoughts, doubts and knowings, and just as long playing jokes and shocking people. Our impish selves had a ball together! Since our voices sounded so similar, we often impersonated each other on the telephone or passed the receiver back and forth during a conversation without the caller ever knowing. For a while we dated the same man, sometimes inviting him on a doubledate—just him and the two of us.

With Peggy I experienced being whole. I could express myself fully all the time and she accepted me unconditionally. This acceptance of my emerging self helped foster a broader self-expression with other people. When Peggy and I parted at the end of our senior year, however, I found I still related to most of the world out of a protective crust, the top two inches of me. Underneath, my inner self remained submerged and silent.

When at last I knew I would go to Philadelphia, I hoped I could be strong enough to express my whole self, even at the risk of being rejected. I saw a new place with new people as a clean slate; my chance to drop my nut image. Being a nut had served its purpose, though at a price, and now I was done with it. Since no one in Philadelphia knew me in that way, there would be no set patterns to limit me. I was determined to express myself from the inside out.

Being in Philadelphia, the actual reality of it, was very different than my fantasy about it before I left Wisconsin. I wasn't prepared for how lonely and depressed I felt. Thrust into a new world away from the secure womb of the university and family, away from my usual mirrors, I lost all but a very dimmed idea of who I was. I missed myself. Without a familiar reflection, the "old" me began to dissipate. Unexpressed aspects of myself battled to surface, challenging the meaninglessness of the outer crust I lived in. For what? I asked, why was I doing this? What was the sense of it all? Struggling to stay afloat in the turmoil, I thrashed about in an infinite sea with nothing to hang on to. Maybe I had made a mistake. Maybe there wasn't a greater reality. Maybe I should just get married, dedicate my life to someone else. Then I wouldn't have to think about making a living or fulfilling some special purpose in life.

My head bobbed up and down in shifting realities. I woke up mornings terrified and nauseated, wanting to pull the covers back over my head and return to unconsciousness. I fought the overwhelming pull of gravity, the extreme heaviness of my being to struggle out of bed, dress myself, and walk to work.

My job, demanding and challenging, forced me to stay focused in present time and was the lifeline that kept me going from day to day. My place in the overall scheme of the workplace, however, was unclear to me and contributed to my confusion. On one hand I was given the responsibility for getting all copy to the production department on time. Delays could cost thousands of dollars. On the other hand, I was asked to sharpen my boss's pencils. Mixed signals from co-workers and my inexperience in work situations made me feel insecure and inadequate. As long as no one told me otherwise, I figured I must be doing okay. I wished, however, for a more precise mirroring to help clarify who I was at the moment.

Alone in my apartment I longed for someone to help sort out my struggle. I lost my spontaneity and sense of humor, and lacked the energy to cultivate friendships. No one in Philadelphia could have guessed I was a nut.

One weekend when I couldn't bare my loneliness any longer, I found newspaper photographs of three people I thought would be good friends for me. I drew their portraits in pastels and hung them on the wall. These were the friends I discussed my feelings with. Each reflected a different perspective and gave me comfort. I also described my struggle in a letter to a friend back in Wisconsin. I had helped him cope with a nervous breakdown years before and hoped he would reciprocate with his wisdom.

There was so much going on within me, I couldn't think it all out. My small Victorian apartment in the converted Governor Pinchot mansion became my workshop for defining the new me. On weekends, I locked the door, took the phone off the hook, and went to it. In between crying jags, I wrote poetry, danced to jazz and classical records, interior-designed my living room, and gave life to sudden inspirations with pastels and watercolors. When the by-product of my inner process, my emotions, came flowing out, I expressed them as works of art. It was effective therapy. My energy slowly returned.

Answering my letter, my Wisconsin friend wrote: "A philosopher once told me, when starting to drown, KEEP SWIMMING!" There is nothing like your own words thrown in your face to slap you back into sanity! I laughed for the first time in an eternity.

At work, I was given a mirror at last: the woman's editor, Miss Dieken, gave me my first three-month evaluation. She was pleased with my effectiveness and encouraged me to be more aggressive. With relief, I knew I was adequate, more than adequate, and had a next step—to be more authoritative.

A trip back home for Easter was the final factor for restoring the sunshine in my life. After hearing that my new job and life in Philadelphia were "fine", the family stopped asking questions. We focused on being together and "doing" the holiday. My inner struggles and conflicts, all my questioning of life— who was I? where was I going?—was out of context here amid the traditional egg hunt, church, and special Easter dinner. Home was always the continual rhythm of a repetitive daily schedule, familiar faces of family and friends, consistent responses to expected actions. Even in my sophisticated Eastern clothes, I was the same ol' Ellen. At another time this would have been frustrating, but this time it was the anchor I needed, a bottom to my sinking. The familiar ground gave me my footing. The confusion I experienced in Philadelphia was far away and unimportant. Here, the mirroring of a familiar image gave me structure and definition. Even if the outer reflection was so different from the inner substance, I was relieved to have something to rest on.

By the time I returned to Philadelphia I was rejuvenated with new energy, hope and motivation. I was ready and eager for whatever was next. Life rushed in again, momentarily pushing the need for answers into a corner. Best of all, my sense of humor returned!

Back at work, one of the first things I did was to paste a paper goldfish on the back of the glass water cooler. Bubbles in the water when someone took a drink made the goldfish appear to be swimming. Laura, my boss, bent over my desk, red-faced with laughter. "You've got to see what someone did to the water cooler!" she cried. "I can't imagine who did it!" Obediently, I ran to the cooler where other staff members had gathered. Laughing with them, I speculated who could have done it. It was the beginning of my new crime wave!

New Horizons

Bonnie, the assistant art director, noticed the difference in me immediately. She began inviting me to her home after work and soon we were close friends. I could be the nut, the serious philosopher, the social gadfly and any of the other me's I wanted to be, and Bonnie would always encourage my expression. When she spotted my pastel friends hanging on the wall of my apartment, she asked to see the rest of my therapy artworks. I was amazed when she insisted I show them to the art director, and even more amazed when he agreed with her that I should do more artistically. Not leaving anything to chance, Bonnie bought me a set of oil paints and gave me my first painting lessons. She was excited about the results, but next to her professional paintings I found mine amateurish. Her praises, however, nurtured my self esteem. I liked the new me Bonnie reflected.

When pantyhose and mini skirts first made their appearance on the fashion scene, Bonnie and I adopted them immediately. We were both ready for a new fashion image. We spent hilarious hours in a wig shop experimenting with various colors and styles of hair. On Bonnie's insistence I walked out with a long, luxuriant frosted-blond fall to augment my fine, mousy-blond, natural hair. Pierced ears were next. Bonnie assured me it was the current fashion trend and set the example by having hers done first. When I gathered enough courage, I arrived on her doorstep with a sharp darning needle and a cork. She gave me a slug of something alcoholic, held an ice cube on my ear for a moment, then shoved the needle through my ear into the cork. Voilá! With the addition of dangling earrings and false eyelashes, I was a modern woman!

Although my workday as assistant to the associate editor was already full, I began accepting writing assignments. Grateful for the chance to write, I didn't mind taking work home. Only after weeks of no social life did I realize I was giving my whole life to *Farm Journal*. Discussing my resentment with Laura was a major breakthrough for me. Always before I felt the need to justify my existence. My innate feelings of inadequacy pushed me to work harder without complaint to accommodate any new demands on me. When Laura agreed to change my responsibilities in order to allow more writing time at the office, I vowed henceforth to set limits on how much time and energy I gave a job. After all, I wasn't living to work. I was working to live! If I was going to live to the fullest, I needed to widen my social horizons. Enlisting another recent arrival to Philadelphia, I began a campaign. We explored the city's parks, museums, restaurants and night spots. We signed up for folk dancing and agreed to be official hostesses for the city. Our commitment to the visitors' center included giving tours of Philadelphia and entertaining foreign visitors in our homes. I learned a great deal about Philadelphia quickly and met a steady stream of interesting people. Before long I began dating a chemist from India who took me to estate parties of the Philadelphia elite and to Washington, D. C., for embassy parties.

It didn't take long to realize the rich exterior of people wasn't always a true reflection of their interiors. At one posh dinner party where everyone sat at a single long table, and the place settings consisted of spoons and forks properly layered around silver plates, the only person who seemed sincerely interested in me as a person was the fashion editor from the city newspaper who sat next to me. Most others greeted me warmly but quickly ran off when they discovered I was a "nobody." One sixtyish matron met me in the women's lounge before dinner. She carried two gowns over her arm. "Oh, my Dear, I'm sooo glad to see you wearing a loooong dress! I didn't know which was appropriate so I brought both a long gown and a short one. Now I know I can wear the looong one." I was glad to be of service, to be the fashion trend setter. I wore the only formal dress I had, one I made myself.

Another man I dated was a young lawyer. He asked me to accompany him to a dinner dance honoring him as a new law firm partner. I was excited and nervous at the prospect of being belle of the ball. When introduced to so many distinguished-looking people, I felt very self-conscious. Then I remembered what Mother told me when I was a teenager. When I felt shy and uncomfortable in large groups of people she reminded me that everyone else was probably feeling the same way. She advised me to focus on helping the other people feel more relaxed.

I kicked off my shoes and began enjoying myself. Suddenly, dance partners seemed to come out of the woodwork. I danced the whole evening without a break. When one of my dance partners commented, "You are so easy to be with and so much fun—its refreshing!" I was astounded. I realized I was fully accepted for being myself!

Even though my social circle was expanding, being spontaneous with my friends was difficult. Bonnie and several others of the *Farm Journal* staff lived close by, but to do something as simple as taking a walk or meeting somewhere for ice cream or for dinner usually took planning. I wished for at least one friend, male or female, to always be "on call"— an instant companion for spur-of-the-moment impulses like going out for a late night snack or running around the block for exercise. I wanted someone I could be totally uninhibited with. It was time to get a roommate.

Finding the right person, it turned out, was easy. My father's cousin called one day to tell me her niece from New Jersey had taken a job in Philadelphia and was looking for a place to live. Although Julie and I had only been together a few times as kids, I remembered the fun we had. As soon as she arrived in town, we agreed she would share my apartment.

Julie had a great sense of humor and was as spontaneous as I was. Our life together was never dull. As soon as we got home from our jobs, we drank double vodka martinis and relaxed in front of the fireplace. Then, while I fixed dinner, Julie entertained me with anecdotes about her job as a social worker, or followed me around the kitchen on her knees singing portions of *Porgy and Bess*. After dinner we smoked cigars and discussed philosophy, or acted on a whim and went out on the town to engage in one hilarious adventure after another. We stimulated each other so much it was hard to stop talking, even after we were in bed with the light off. We had to agree to be quiet so we could get some sleep.

Every other weekend Julie left to visit the man she was engaged to, her "paramour," who lived in New Jersey. I used this time alone to examine my current state of being: what I liked or didn't like about myself, my progress in expressing the true me. When I kept active and focused in the present moment, all was fine, but in solitude the old feelings of purposelessness and doubt resurfaced. Thoughts of the future frightened me.

Even before leaving Wisconsin I knew I would be in Philadelphia for just two years. After that, I had no feeling about what should occur. The unknowing gnawed in me and, at times, my depression returned. When I looked ahead, my future was hollow, devoid of meaning, and barren. Even though I felt I had a special purpose in life, there had been no outer confirmation of that fact. Just to live to live seemed senseless, no matter how much I enjoyed life. For now, however, there was no alternative. I could retreat— go home if I wanted to—but I didn't want to go back. I had voluntarily burned the bridges to my past. The only way to go was forward.

Jack

With delight, I learned Philadelphia maintained over a hundred miles of connected riding trails throughout its park system. One Sunday morning I inquired about the nearest riding stable and found a bus to take me there. Although riding horses was a childhood passion of mine, I rode infrequently and never developed confidence. My unfulfilled dream was to gallop through flowered meadows with nothing to stop me but the resistance of the wind. Arriving at the stable, I walked up to the barn and was met by the owner. When I asked about riding lessons, he quickly introduced his friend Jack, standing close by.

I followed Jack to another barn to meet his handsome and enormous palomino, Tiger. The horse's name and immense size immediately intimidated me and my emotions must have been displayed on my face. Jack assured me Tiger was a very gentle horse, just spirited! With these encouraging words and with

Jack's help, I pulled myself onto Tiger's back. After a few uneventful walks around the ring, I relaxed, and patted Tiger's neck to acknowledge our new friendship.

At the end of my first lesson, I asked Jack how many other students he had. None, he informed me, I was his first and only student, ever. When he saw me approaching the stable that morning, he had quickly informed the stable owner he would teach me if I wanted lessons!

We met at the stables every Sunday morning from then on. Jack patiently taught me the basics of English riding while Tiger cooperated beautifully. The more confident I became, the more they both challenged me. Tiger seemed to sense my level of competency and gave me more to handle as I improved, gradually testing my skill by waiting for my precise signals before responding. With such excellent tutors, I was soon ready to ride the trails. Since Tiger was Jack's horse, it was natural that Jack would ride him and rent another horse for me. Only when we were on the trail, however, did the real reasons become obvious why Jack, not me, rode Tiger, and why Tiger was called Tiger. No longer the gentle, compliant horse of the ring, Tiger pulled ahead to go, go, go! If Jack tried to rein him in, he objected and balked—snorting and rearing—making Jack work hard to keep him under control. The open trail seemed to induce the same impulse in Tiger that it did in me—the desire to fly!

Our Sunday mornings from then on began with a short trail ride down to the Schuylkill River and then a long and satisfying canter to our destination— an old picturesque inn where we liked to eat breakfast. Jack's friends, wearing traditional riding habits, accompanied us on magnificent thoroughbred horses. The whole scene was one I had previously drooled over in New England travel folders. Now I was part of it. Gaping like a little kid, I took in every nuance while trying to appear nonchalant and experienced. Jack's gentle manner, sense of humor, and sincere interest in people helped put me at ease and brought a unifying cordiality to the party. After breakfast Jack and I usually split off from the group to spend the rest of the day traversing the back trails by ourselves.

Jack's love for the outdoors and his joy of riding on crisp fall days matched mine. We rode for hours in almost complete silence, our rare conversation being about horses and riding, nothing personal. Even after several months of riding together, Jack had told me very little about himself except that he and his brothers had a large produce business that supplied local restaurants with fresh fruits and vegetables. Other riders informed me he was very wealthy and well respected. It wasn't his personal life that interested me, anyway. It was the wonderful way he related to people, his total enjoyment of life, and the respectful relationship he had with his horse that I noticed, and that made me trust Jack completely.

One Sunday when I arrived at the stable later than usual, a horse had been reserved for me, but Jack had gone on to have breakfast with the rest of the gang. Alone, I rode down the trail feeling very odd. It just wasn't the same without Jack. I missed him. Suddenly, as I descended the hill to the river, Jack and Tiger appeared below me—a magnificent picture! My heart froze. Jack led Tiger up to me and turned around beside me. He seemed very happy to see me. It was mutual. Jack and I rode in our usual silence the rest of the afternoon, but something had changed between us. When Jack invited me out for dinner with him that evening, I accepted.

For the next few weeks Jack wined and dined me frequently at all the restaurants he serviced through his business, displaying me proudly to his friends. We were treated royally wherever we went, making me feel very pampered and womanly.

Driving home one night, Jack stopped the car and said he wanted to talk. He told me how wonderful the past few weeks had been, and then, as gently as he could, informed me he was married and had four kids, the youngest son being my age. I nearly fainted—but anger revived me quickly. Being inexperienced with older men, I never thought to ask about Jack's marital status. Besides, I trusted him. When I told Jack how upset I was not to have this bit of information when he first asked me out, he apologized and begged me to trust him. He didn't want to explain his marital situation, but assured me I wouldn't be in any jeopardy because of it. He felt I needed to know he was married only now that we were seeing more of each other. He had been afraid that if he told me before, I wouldn't go out with him. He was right, of course, and now that we had a fondness between us, it would be harder for me to refuse. I quickly rationalized: in the several months we had known each other, Jack had never expressed his feelings for me, never pushed, never asked me for anything. My mind reached the same conclusion my heart did: keep trusting!

We continued to ride on Sundays but now Jack picked me up at my apartment first so we could eat breakfast together before going to the stable. We still rode with the group, but not as often. Jack bragged about my riding and made sure I was the first to ride any new horse the stable acquired. Even I was amazed at my ability to conquer the quirkiest of the horses, the difficult ones no one else wanted to ride.

Jack's confidence in me gave me confidence in myself. When Jack decided I was ready to ride Tiger outside the ring, however, I questioned his sanity! He prodded me until I finally consented to try. I should have listened to my instincts. No sooner had I mounted and we were outside the confinement of the ring, than Tiger bolted and took off at top speed. Nothing I could say or do had any influence on him. Stubbornly persisting, he charged toward some destination he obviously had in mind. There was nothing for me to do except hang on until Jack could catch up to us on another horse and grab the reins. This experience should have been enough for all three of us, but Jack's determination to have me master Tiger only doubled.

One Sunday he asked if I wanted to learn how to jump. Did I! Jumping on a horse was just one step away from galloping unrestrained through flowered meadows! I consented once again to Jack's whim of learning on Tiger. As long as we were in the ring I would be safe. Jack set up some low jumps and rode Tiger over them to show me how easy it was. I mounted Tiger eagerly and listened closely to Jack's instructions. I led Tiger successfully over the first jump and stopped before attempting the second. When I reined him in long enough to catch my breath, Tiger balked at the restraint. When I pulled harder, Tiger objected and reared—again, and again. Jack's face went ashen white as he watched Tiger totally out of control trying to squash me against a truck in the corral. Helplessly hanging on for dear life, I suddenly remembered what my college sailing instructor told me when my boat gusted out of control in a strong wind: Let go and let the boat right itself. I let the rein slacken, relaxed my body and clung onto Tiger's mane. It worked! Tiger stopped fighting and quieted down with me still on his back. Relieved, Jack grabbed me down from the saddle and held me close. He yelled at Tiger, the first and only time I had heard him raise his voice to his horse, and praised me for not panicking.

Jack's affection for me increased. He asked me to be with him constantly. Although I cared for him deeply, I didn't love him the way he said he loved me. I enjoyed his company and our riding together, but Jack was twice my age (and married!), and at the moment I wasn't interested in being with only one man. There was still a big world to explore. I began to pull away.

When one of my co-workers at *Farm Journal* announced she was getting married, I looked forward to going to the wedding. Weddings were always fun and a great place to meet new people, especially men. Four of us from the staff agreed to drive up together to Mystic, Connecticut, the place the bride and groom-to-be had picked off the map for their ceremony. Neither of them had ever been there before—they did all the arranging for the event on the telephone.

In the car on the way up the night before the wedding, I announced to my friends I wanted to swim in the pool as soon as we arrived at our motel. Everyone laughed at the idea. Going swimming wasn't the foremost thought in their minds—I was the only one who brought a suit. Unfortunately, by the time we checked into the Holiday Inn, it was too late to go swimming, pool hours were over. Disappointed, I accompanied the other women to the cocktail lounge.

When we walked in—four spirited young women up for a good time—we captured everyone's attention. On the way to our table I especially noticed a man who half-turned from the bar to give us a glance. Something about his eyes struck me as being unusual.

Our drinks were served and we gaily toasted the bride-to-be. An over-inebriated man wanting to be a little too friendly leaned on our table. Two men from the next table helped steer him away. We invited an older couple who wanted to know more about Philadelphia to join us and gradually things quieted down.

Sometime later I happened to look toward the bar and see the man with the unusual eyes suddenly stand up and begin to go table to table. When people at one table shook their heads at him, he passed on to the next table. Finally, he came to us. "Anyone want to go swimming?" he asked. When I informed him the pool was closed, he said he had requested special permission. We could swim at our own risk. When I was the only one to take him up on his offer, we agreed to meet at the pool.

Glancing out the window of our room as I pulled my suit on, I could just see the pool where my swimming friend was taking off his trousers. "Oh my gosh! He doesn't have a suit on!" I exclaimed to my giggling companions who all rushed to the window to get a better look. It was too dark to see clearly but we agreed he must have something on. I grabbed my towel and went down to the pool to join him.

He was already in the water as I slipped in. He introduced himself as "Jack." We exchanged small talk as we passed each other in our laps. "You married? he asked.

"Yes," I replied without thinking, then wondered why I lied.

"You?" I asked.

"Nope," he said.

Jack had come from New Haven for a drink. He hadn't been swimming in ten years and had no idea what had possessed him. Suddenly he had an overwhelming desire to swim! I told him how I had planned to go even before I left Philadelphia and how disappointed I was to find the pool closed.

After a half an hour of swimming laps, Jack asked if I wanted to get some coffee. I agreed. He waited for me to climb out of the pool before asking me to turn around—he wasn't wearing a suit! When he was dressed we went into the motel's coffee shop.

We ordered our coffee and waited in silence to be served. Jack laughed self-consciously and then confessed he was married after all. Why he had told me he wasn't, he didn't know. It was my turn to laugh— I informed him I wasn't married and didn't know why I had told him I was! Jack became very silent as he studied me with his big wise eyes. "Something very strange is happening here," he said. "I feel as if I've known you all my life and yet I know nothing about you." Indeed, I was experiencing the same phenomenon. As we inquired about each other's lives we found much to talk about. In fact, we were so engrossed in conversation, we completely forgot about time. Jack first checked his watch at 6:00 A.M.!

The sun came up as Jack walked me to my room. He told me how much our meeting had meant to him, how he communicated so easily and so intimately with me, expressing many things he hadn't even shared with his wife. The experience was mutual. I had shared my deepest feelings with him and felt he was one of the few people who seemed to understand me completely. It had been a wonderful evening, but when we hugged good-by I never thought to question whether we would see each other again. My mind was already racing ahead, anticipating the excitement of the wedding.

Monday morning I couldn't settle down to work. I sat at my desk reviewing the events of the weekend in my mind. When the phone rang I answered it automatically. "Thank goodness I found you!" a voice said, startling me out of my reverie. It was Jack from Connecticut! "I've been thinking about you all weekend and realized I didn't have your phone number," he went on. "At least I remembered where you worked! I really want to talk to you again. Will you meet me in New York for dinner Friday night?"

The warning lights flashed bright red in my head. "No," I told him.

"Because I'm married?" he asked.

"Yes," I admitted, and explained how I was already involved with one married man, also named Jack, and that was enough. I didn't want to repeat the experience.

"I'm not asking you to have an affair with me," he replied, "just talk. If you come to New York and then don't feel comfortable, you can always turn around and go home."

It seemed rational and safe enough. "Okay," I consented. When I hung up the phone I excitedly rushed to tell the other women who had shared the weekend. As the week passed, however, my stomach let me know that something inside me wasn't fully convinced this was as safe a venture as my logical mind had concluded. My mind won out. Friday after work I headed for the train station.

Riding the escalator down to the track, I arrived on the platform sweating and flushed. I put my suitcase down to unbutton my coat. Suddenly, all my doubts caught up to me. How silly could I be, running off to New York to meet a man I only met once. True, we covered a lot of ground in that one meeting, but really, what did I know about him? Panic gripped me. I grabbed my bag and about-faced in attempt to bolt home. I didn't get far—a young man blocked my way. "Could you tell me what time it is?" he asked, grinning broadly. I held up my wrist so he could see my watch and tried once again to dash away. "Where are you going?" the stranger stood his ground.

"New York," I answered congenially, as any polite Midwesterner would, but under the circumstances my heart wasn't in it. It was busy overloading my head with blood, thumping out the question: will I go or won't I? The young man's next words were totally lost on me as I anxiously riveted my attention ahead on the up escalator.

Then I spotted something I recognized—some very familiar grey-blue eyes peering at me from around a post. New Haven Jack smiled sheepishly as his dapper body slowly joined his face in full view. I stared at him dumbfounded. I was trapped! There was no question of running now.

Jack picked up my bag and gently steered me toward the train without a bit of resistance from me. Weak with shock, I could hardly walk. We boarded the train and Jack guided me to the parlor car, where he had reserved seats. Within minutes we were sitting across from each other.

While I stared speechlessly at him, Jack smiled and joked about my being "picked up" by another man. Then, growing very serious, he explained his unexpected presence in Philadelphia: "As zero hour approached and I anticipated our meeting in New York, I knew if you were feeling even a fraction of what I was feeling you would never get on the train. I don't know what is going on, but I know it is important. I feel compelled to follow it through no matter what. I came here to make sure you got on the train."

Slowly recovering my senses, I assessed the situation. Was I being duped? "Did you reserve one hotel room or two?" I asked. Jack laughed and assured me I had my own room. His innocent and twinkling grey-blue eyes quieted my suspicions. I relaxed and we quickly slipped into the same intimacy we experienced the first time we met.

As we talked, something very odd began happening physically. At first I felt drugged. Then I experienced a curious sense of floating out of my seat with no consciousness of my body at all. I bobbed along the ceiling, my voice seeming far off and not mine. When I told Jack what was happening, he said he was experiencing a similar phenomenon. The world around us faded. All I could see were Jack's eyes staring into mine, his voice coming from somewhere in the distance. Only when the other passengers in the car began to stand up and file out did we suddenly become aware of our bodies again and know we had arrived in New York. It took a few minutes to realize where we were and to begin to function normally again, as if abruptly awakening from a deep sleep.

We took a cab to our hotel and checked into our rooms—our separate rooms. As soon as I was settled I went to meet Jack in the cocktail lounge. He waved to me from the revolving bar and waited for me to join him and order my drink. Then he held up his wallet and said he wanted to show me something. One by one he displayed the pictures of his four children! Before, in Connecticut, when I asked him about children, he said he didn't have any. I asked him if there were any more lies he needed to confess. He said that was the last one.

Jack was thirty, six years older than I was, and something of a financial genius. When he started his own bank with new progressive methods, he had been mentioned with his picture in *Time* magazine. Since then he had sold out to his partner, worked for Chase Manhattan, then joined the investment firm where he was currently employed. Everything was going well for him. He loved his wife and took pride in being a good provider for his family. So why, he asked, was he feeling depressed and lonely lately, and why was he so compelled to be with me? Neither of us knew the answers.

In the elevator on the way to dinner, I caught Jack looking at me in a very odd way. "God!" he said, "you are such an iceberg!" I was shocked and hurt. I thought of myself as a warm and affectionate person. But that's not what he meant. "All I can see of you is the tip," he explained. "There is so much more below the surface you aren't showing. I want to see all of it!"

Something gave way inside of me. I was confused and excited at the same time. I felt exposed and vulnerable, yet relieved someone was finally seeing me—the inner as well as the outer. Over dinner and late into the night we talked, exploring our feelings, our thoughts and our observations about each other.

Later in bed, I tossed and turned, my mind racing as fast as my emotions churned. A floodgate had opened. I rushed outward, released at last of my previously limited self-image. Parts of me flowed in all directions, seeking new boundaries, a new identity. Who was I really? I felt both wonderful and frightened. A new sense of self was surfacing. I was coming alive. All of this because of Jack. I felt so close to him, as if we were joined somehow, and part of each other.

My heart ached and after hours of resisting the thought, I finally admitted to myself that I LOVED this man. I jumped out of bed, resolved to tell him so.

Once before I loved a man and never told him because for some reason I felt you should only declare love to someone you intended to marry. I had since realized how silly this was, that love was too precious not to be expressed. I had vowed that if I ever loved again, I would tell the person my feelings. The time had come. I couldn't wait until morning. I opened the door joining our two rooms and woke up Jack. I told a completely flabbergasted man I loved him. Hugging him tightly, I wanted to hold him forever and never let go.

It was difficult saying good-by the next day. There was no telling when we would see each other again, even though Jack promised to come to Philadelphia as soon as he could manage it. I sat in a trance all the way back to Philadelphia, reliving every detail of the weekend over and over again in my mind, trying to convince myself this was real, not a dream.

Jack #2

I chose not to mention Jack #2 (my designation for keeping my Jacks straight) to Jack #1. I needed time to sort out my newly complicated life, make some sense of it all, and decide where I was headed. Although his place from the forefront of my life had slipped, I was fond of Jack and treasured our time together. I didn't know how he would react to knowing about another important man in my life and I didn't want to hurt him.

Out of the blue, Jack asked if I had ever been to an astrologer. "A what?" I asked. He laughed at my puzzled expression and explained that an astrologer was someone who could tell me much about myself and my life by calculating the position of the planets when I was born. Skeptical, but curious, I agreed to go for a reading. I didn't dare hope someone who didn't know me could decipher the strange bent my life was taking.

A week later, Jack accompanied me to my appointment with the astrologer. To make sure I wouldn't give clues about myself from my appearance or occupation, I dressed nondescriptly and asked Jack to introduce me as a secretary. When the astrologer, a tall, older woman, answered the door and welcomed us warmly, I liked her immediately. We sat at a small table while she showed me the astrological chart she had prepared using my birth time, place, and date. She explained how the numbers and odd symbols indicated different things depending on their placement in the chart. By "reading" the chart, she summarized my life from birth to the present, telling me things about myself that no one else knew. I was surprised and amazed with the accuracy of her information.

After serving tea and cookies she proceeded to tell me what the chart said about my future: if I wasn't already writing I soon would be; in February of the next year I would move toward the ocean; that an older man would ask me to marry him but I wouldn't; and that I would meet a man my own age, marry him and have one mystical child. I was flabbergasted! But that wasn't the end. The astrologer looked curiously at me, then Jack, before saying, "There is something here that perhaps would be better to tell you in private." I assured her it was all right to say anything with Jack present. "I see that you are secretly seeing a man that you have met recently and have a strong connection with." Jack gave me a surprised look as I nodded affirmatively. I gave the astrologer Jack #2's birth date and place so she could calculate a quick chart for him and compare it to mine. She informed me that ours was the strongest possible relationship that a man and woman could have, that our astrological charts were two halves of a complete whole. My heart beat rapidly when she told me this and nearly stopped altogether when she looked me straight in the eye and said, "This relationship will not be beneficial for you if you stay in it too long. At some point you must pull yourself out of it, no matter how hard it is. Otherwise, you will not accomplish what you came into this world to do."

On the way home, Jack and I had quite a talk! I told him more about Jack #2 and how I was uncertain what to do about him, especially so because he was married. Jack was very understanding and encouraged me to follow my heart—you never know where it will lead. Then, finally, he explained his own marital situation. When his son died a tragic death five years before, his wife had been admitted into a mental hospital where she had remained ever since. There wasn't much left of their relationship, much less their marriage. He hadn't wanted me to know this before because he didn't want me to be with him out of pity. He hoped I would marry him. Though I cared deeply for him, I knew I didn't love him. We agreed to continue our friendship and keep riding together.

Jack #2 arranged a "business trip" to Philadelphia several weeks after our meeting in New York. I waited impatiently for his arrival, wondering if he would look the way I remembered him. As soon as the door buzzer indicated Jack was at the entrance to the apartment building, I pressed the button releasing the locked door, and rushed out into the hallway. Hanging over the railing, I watched Jack ascend the circular staircase to the third floor. I called down to him. He looked up and smiled. "Hello!" he said. He was even more handsome than I remembered.

Immediately, the deep intimacy was there between us. For the next two days we talked incessantly, taking time out only to eat and sleep. The rest of the world disappeared and the strange physical sensations we experienced on the train to New York recurred. Whenever we were alone talking to each other, I felt my head disconnect from my body and float upward. Jack's eyes appeared in front of me near the ceiling. Our voices sounded far away. Although this was an uncomfortable experience, I was beginning to get used to it. What I couldn't handle was Jack calling home to check in with his wife. The lies he told her made me feel terrible and I ran into the bedroom until Jack was off the phone. He was upset, too. We felt guilty but wanted to be together. What should we do? At the end of the weekend we decided we each needed to think and feel out our situation separately. We agreed to a two-week silence during which we wouldn't phone or see each other. Jack would then return to Philadelphia and we would make a decision whether or not to pursue the relationship.

Without hearing from Jack, the next two weeks dragged on endlessly. Try as I might, I couldn't come up with any new thoughts or clear answers for myself. It was an endless circle: I loved Jack and wanted to be with him; he loved me, too, but was married and also loved his wife; we felt guilty but wanted to be together. Since I couldn't come up with a clear solution, I hoped Jack would. When Friday of the second week finally came, I began to sing! At work, all I could think of was that Jack would be there that night.

When my office phone rang late in the afternoon, it was Jack. He sounded terrible. "There's a special delivery letter in your mailbox from me. I'm not coming tonight. The letter will explain in detail, but in essence it says that I'm afraid if I come tonight, I will never leave."

I hung up the phone and ran to the restroom, crying uncontrollably. For the remainder of the afternoon I struggled to finish a photography session without displaying my emotional turmoil. I experienced an overwhelming sense of loss, as if someone close to me had died. My heart was so heavy I could barely get my body to move.

The thought of going back to an empty apartment (Julie had left for the weekend) and to the letter from Jack was unbearable. I took a long detour home, hoping the bustling activity of Market Street would be distracting. Usually there were enough poor souls hanging around to remind me how fortunate I was, no matter what was bothering me. It didn't work this time. I was too numb with pain to notice anyone else.

Zombie-like, I plodded up the front stairs of the apartment building. Turning to go in, I heard the toot of a horn—a car rushed up to the curb and stopped. Two sad, grey-blue eyes looked out at me. Without a word, I ran to the car and got in. Jack and I clung to each other and cried.

After telling me he wasn't coming, Jack said he was engulfed with grief. He knew then that whatever was going on between us was too powerful and important not to be explored. We would have to put our guilt aside and let our relationship, whatever it was, unfold. His decision made, he drove maniacally from New Haven to Philadelphia to tell me.

What joy! We danced down the streets that night, the world bright and perfect. When Jack left Sunday night, half of me went with him.

We talked on the phone every evening. I sprawled out on the kitchen table with a box of Kleenex. My moods, yo-yoing between joy and sadness, created a steady flow of tears. Never before had my emotions been so out of control. It was frightening...and intoxicating. My friends commented on how beautiful I looked —it must be love! Every cell of me came alive.

Jack made as many trips to Philadelphia as he could manage without raising suspicions at home, but more often I met him in New Haven. I took the train after work on Fridays, checked into the Hotel Sheraton and waited. Jack came as soon as he could.

I loved to jump into his lap and prattle on and on nonstop about my week's activities and thoughts. Jack listened attentively, his eyes—caverns of wisdom and infinite patience—locked in on mine. Gradually, I stopped talking and looked to Jack expectantly. He would smile and then say something totally unrelated to what I was saying. It would summarize exactly what was going on with me, or with us. Immediately, the conversation plunged to a deeper level. The world fell away and our disconnected heads bobbed on the ceiling. Our energies pooled together, blending our souls in a kind of lovemaking—each of us becoming more of the other and more of ourselves. Suddenly, we would be aware of our bodies and the room again, the world looking fresh and clear.

Sometimes Jack pointed out I wasn't saying what I was really thinking. When I insisted I was, he stood his ground and got me so angry I would finally say what I truly thought—much to my own surprise! Little by little Jack coaxed the submerged part of the iceberg to surface, a part of me I didn't even know existed. The discovery was exhilarating.

Occasionally, on our weekends together, we took long rides through the Connecticut countryside. Jack told stories of his boyhood and serenaded me with Irish love songs, or we talked about what we wanted in life. It was Jack's dream to buy us a sailboat and sail around the world. He surprised me one day by driving to the marina to show me the "perfect" sailboat for us. After a great deal of research he picked

out the safest sailboat he could find. It was ugly! I
told him it looked like a bathtub. He never mentioned
sailing again.

I didn't mean to hurt him, but Jack's eternal vigi-
lance in making sure I was safe often blinded his sense
of aesthetics. For me, many of the safety features of
things he chose were a burden and limited my spontaneity. This was a major difference in our natures. I
always plunged into whatever felt right at the moment, whereas he researched each move before taking a step. The biggest incongruence with his usual
pattern, he said, was me. He insisted our relationship
was making him into a looney!

At first he was embarrassed by my skipping
down the street when I was happy—which was often
when I was with him—and he called me his "little
hippie," referring to my colorful way of dress and
ease of showing affection. Gradually, by osmosis, he
picked up some of my habits, becoming more effu-
sive and prone to dancing down the street with me.

One Saturday morning, I watched from my hotel window for Jack's car to drive up the parking garage ramp below me. When I spotted him, I stood up
on the window ledge and pressed myself full length
to the glass. Jack spotted my red dress immediately.
The play began. He stopped on every turn of the ramp
throwing kisses, and I danced in the window blow-
ing kisses back. He parked the car on the roof of the
garage, got out and began dancing, bowing, and tip-
ping his hat to me. I laughed so hard I lost my balance and fell off the ledge into the room. Later, when

we were together, Jack exclaimed, "Now I know I've flipped!"

Late one night when I returned to my apartment in Philadelphia after having a good time with a friend, I was seized with overwhelming emotion. I fell onto the couch, crying uncontrollably. After several minutes the emotion receded. Bewildered, I waited a moment before undressing for bed. As I entered the bedroom, it struck again. I quickly muffled my sobbing with a pillow, but it was too late. Julie was already awake and had her arms around me. Between sobs I tried to explain what was happening—something must be wrong with Jack! I had to call him! Hysterically, I groped for the light. Julie informed me it was 3:15 A.M. I couldn't call Jack—he'd think I was crazy! Gradually, I quieted down. Julie joked and I began to laugh. I was totally mystified.

At 8:00 the next morning, the phone rang. Jack greeted me, "What happened to you around 3:00 last night?" I played dumb and asked him why he wanted to know. He told me he had suddenly awakened and was gripped with fear as he saw a red tombstone appear in front of him. He ran to the telephone knowing I was in some kind of danger. As he dialed my number he glanced at the clock—3 A.M.! He quickly came to his senses. He couldn't call me, I'd think he was crazy!

It became increasingly obvious that the bond between Jack and myself was strong and unusual. We accepted the strange events that occurred as part of the magic between us. Even when I wasn't home, I knew when Jack was trying to call me. I would suddenly hear a phone ringing in my head and know Jack was letting the phone ring in my apartment. I would write down the time when I felt him call and ask him about it later. I was always right. This, and the experience of having the train station we were sitting in suddenly appear to us as a steepled cathedral, had no other explanation except being evidence of our love. The weird part was when our magic began to show!

We were in the Hotel Sheraton cocktail lounge having a drink before dinner. The band started to play and Jack asked me to dance. Totally enthralled with each other, we didn't notice anyone else. When the music stopped we stood still, holding each other for a moment. Then, suddenly, we realized we were the only ones on the dance floor. Everyone else had gathered around the sidelines and was gawking at us. Not knowing what was going on, we stood there and stared back. A woman ran up to us, touched me on the arm, and withdrew her hand quickly. "Don't you know you are glowing?" she exclaimed. "There is a ring of green light around you!" As soon as we noticed the clear green light engulfing us, it began to disappear. It appeared one other time— when we were walking down the street. People jumped away from us, gasping, "Yikes! You're glowing!"

A Voice

Two years after moving to Philadelphia, I felt restless. I had conquered the major difficulties of my job and wanted a new challenge. In assessing my chances for a better editorial position at *Farm Journal*, I realized there was nowhere to go—the possibility of one of the editors leaving soon was slim. It was time to find a new job. Instead of telling anyone I was looking (I didn't want to hurt my chances for a raise), I just kept my ears open and attuned to the publishing network. I didn't have a particular location or job in mind, I only knew that I wanted to be in a creative position where I could write and work with people.

Late one afternoon when most everyone had left the office, I was sitting at my desk pondering the situation. Since nothing significant had turned up on its own, I was considering some active inquiring. Suddenly, a very distinct voice said, "Wait one month!" Startled, I looked around—no one was there. I looked out in the hall. Again, no one. Why should I wait one month? I asked silently. Even though no one answered, whoever or whatever it was that spoke to me did so with such authority I couldn't ignore the advice. I decided to wait the month before I went looking for a new job.

Exactly one month later I received a letter from the National Dairy Council. I had interviewed for a job with them in Wisconsin two years before. They still had my résumé on file and wanted to inform me of two positions available, one in Philadelphia and another in Boston. Within a day or two I received a second unsolicited letter advising me of a third job opening in Pittsburgh. The message was clear, the time was now! I called about the job that appealed to me most, a public relations position with the New England Dairy and Food Council in Boston. The job included developing and demonstrating recipes using dairy products, writing media releases, and being the TV and radio personality for the dairy industry. It sounded like just the challenge I was looking for. I arranged to be interviewed immediately.

When I informed Jack I was applying for a job in Boston, he urged me to look in New Haven instead. Boston, he reasoned, was just as far from him as Philadelphia. He offered to buy me a house in New Haven and train me as a financial advisor so I could work with him. Even though the thought of living closer to Jack was appealing, working as a financial advisor was not my cup of tea. When I turned him down, Jack said the least I could do, then, was to spend a day or two in New Haven on my way to Boston. I agreed, and, without letting anyone, except Bonnie, know my intentions, requested vacation time for my trip. I decided to use my time in New Haven to assemble a portfolio containing examples of my editing and writing experience, and asked Jack to reserve a big enough hotel room for me to spread out my work. I knew I would get claustrophobic if I had to spend three days in a little room filled with papers.

When I arrived at the Sheraton in New Haven I was informed a convention suite had been reserved for me. I said there must be some mistake. The reservations clerk repeated my name and the dates I needed the room. Correct. Then I laughed, realizing this must be Jack's idea of a joke. I laughed even harder when I saw the suite. The bedroom was enormous, not to mention the size of the adjoining conference room! Even Jack was surprised at the size of the rooms. He agreed to help make use of them as often as he could. Whenever he could be away from job and family, he came to be with me. He did whatever he could to convince me I needed to live in New Haven, but remembering the astrologer's warning about staying too long in a relationship with Jack and not doing what I came into the world to do helped me resist any temptation I felt.

My first view of Boston, framed by the taxi cab's window, unexpectedly gave me a "coming home" feeling. I was totally charmed by the Boston

Commons, the State house, the narrow streets and the liveliness of the people. The feeling expanded with my meeting the executive director of the Dairy Council. She was warm, direct and had a great sense of humor. I knew I could work well with her and sensed she felt the same about me. On the way back to the train station a deep sense of peace ebbed in me. I knew the job was mine if I wanted it and I let myself fully experience what this new life could be. The only hole in my balloon was Jack.

All the way back to Philadelphia my thoughts played havoc with my emotions. Jack felt so strongly about me coming to live in New Haven and was offering me the emotional and financial security I thought I always wanted. If we were ever going to live closer together this would be the time. It would be wonderful not to feel emotionally halved all the time—the way I felt when Jack and I didn't see each other often enough. Yet, when I imagined myself in the position of "being taken care of," I knew it wasn't for me—part of me would be restless and unfulfilled. I knew there was something I was to do in life that couldn't happen in New Haven. But, then, what could I tell Jack so he would know how much I loved him and still understand that it would be stifling for me to live in New Haven?

It was hard to focus on my work the next couple of days. I kept wondering what I would do if I got the job. What would I do if I didn't? I was relieved when the waiting was over and I was offered the position at the salary and benefits I had asked for. Instead of accepting the job right away, however, I told the executive director of the Dairy Council I would give her my answer the next day, and immediately called Jack with the news. I wanted him to feel good about my accepting the job before I made the final decision. It was an emotional conversation, and I hung up feeling completely drained.

I slept restlessly that night and arrived at work early the next morning, still unclear about what to do. As I settled down at my desk with a cup of coffee, the phone rang. It was Jack. "Take the job," he said cheerfully. "It will be great for you! I'm sorry I've been so selfish. I really want you to grow and be happy. We'll work something out. I love you."

I hung up the phone and ran to the art department to share the news with Bonnie. As soon as I went back to my desk, I called the Dairy Council and accepted the position. No sooner had I put the receiver down when Laura arrived. Walking briskly past my desk she said to please follow her into her inner office immediately. Looking very grave she asked me to shut the door and have a seat.

It took her a few moments to begin. It was rare when Laura was at a loss for words. "I don't know how to tell you this," she began. "You have been an excellent assistant and I don't know how I could do without you. As you know, we have a new editor who is making some radical changes. He is completely reorganizing everything and cutting back our staff.

He is letting people go who have been here 25 years! I'm afraid that your position is one that he is eliminating."

I couldn't believe my ears or what was happening! Laura went on to explain more about the reorganization plan and how everything would be done to help those who were leaving to relocate. It would be especially difficult for some of the new assistants who had just made long moves to work there. For me, I could take as much time in the next two weeks as needed to interview for other jobs, and I would be given an extra two week's salary in addition to whatever else I had coming to me.

How exquisitely perfect the timing of the universe was! I couldn't believe how everything was working out so miraculously for me. Laura ran out of words and looked at me expectantly. It was my turn to talk. I wanted to make her feel better. "Don't worry, Laura," I said, "I just accepted a job in Boston." Her reaction was of shock, relief and curiosity. When I told her all that had happened we both laughed and cried from the release of tension.

Boston

The first prediction of the astrologer proved to be true. I moved to Boston, on the ocean, in February to begin my work at the New England Dairy and Food Council. While I temporarily quartered in a motel, Jack came up from New Haven to help me find a "safe" place to live. His idea of safe was a guarded castle with a moat around it. He picked a penthouse in an expensive security apartment complex. The high rental price, he said, was worth the peace of mind it would give him. He would gladly pay the difference from what I felt I could afford. This situation was not at all what I had in mind. Tactfully, I informed Jack that the location wasn't practical—I would have to take two subways to get to work.

As soon as Jack left for home, I looked on my own and quickly found just what I wanted, a one bedroom apartment with a balcony overlooking an inner courtyard, for $225 a month. Best of all, it was within walking distance of work. When I reported my find to my new fellow workers at the Dairy Council, they recounted their individual trials of trying to find a decent place to live in Boston at a reasonable price. I had apparently accomplished the impossible by finding such a deal so quickly.

My orientation at the Dairy Council was brief. Miss Bridges, the executive director, explained my responsibilities but then apologized for being at a loss as to how I was to carry them out. There had been a long lapse between my predecessor, Janet, and myself. No one really knew how she did what she did because she had been there nine years after creating the job herself, and never wrote anything down. The only thing Miss Bridges could tell me, as she went out the door for a month's vacation, was that she thought I was scheduled to do a TV appearance in two weeks!

A TV appearance? What did that mean? I asked my co-workers, but no one was sure—only that Janet did a TV show every two weeks on one of the major networks. I quickly made some phone calls and found that, indeed, I was scheduled to be completely responsible for the 15-minute show in two weeks. Even though I had appeared on TV before—with the girl scouts, various school events, and the church choir— I had never been *responsible* for a show. I had planned and played out a show in front of my journalism class in college, but this was different, it was *real*!

I panicked and called Janet where she was currently employed. She tried to calm me down, saying it was easy—I would do fine. I wasn't convinced and begged her to come to dinner the next evening. Since my furnishings hadn't yet arrived from Philadelphia, I had to make do. I fed the food editor from Boston's second largest newspaper day-old spaghetti with the only fork I owned (I ate with a spoon). We sat on borrowed chairs around a cardboard box table.

Janet persisted in making light of my fears about the TV show and suggested that I start with something I knew enough about and that would take little preparation. The goal, she reminded me, was to educate about good nutrition while subtly promoting dairy products. By the end of the evening she succeeded in making me feel that the task was perhaps possible and that, indeed, I could carry it out successfully.

Once I decided on the topic, "What Makes a Good Breakfast," I let my creativity take over and enjoyed the preparation. My nervousness increased, however, the closer my taping time came. I barely ate for several days prior to the show. The DAY arrived and somehow even with all my stage fright I managed to get to the studio on time. I was immediately informed that the host of the show had died that day. He had been terminally ill and his frequent substitute during the progression of his illness was to be his successor. I was his first guest!

I proudly handed Kent a complete script of what he should say and what I would say—just as my journalism training had taught me to do—and gave the camera crew a written rundown of the close-up shots I wanted. Since I had thoroughly planned this out, I knew that if all I had to do was follow the script, I would be all right. Impromptu speaking terrified me.

Kent and I sat in our swivel chairs, adjusted our microphones and waited for the ON-camera signal from the crew. My opening shot was a cheeseburger, a perfect, well balanced breakfast. The tension of the moment stopped the blood flowing in my veins. This was it . . . we were on! Kent started talking. Unfortunately, the blood in my head was drumming too loudly for me to hear very well. Kent stopped talking and looked at me. I realized he had asked me a question, a question that was *not on the script!* This I couldn't handle. I zipped out of my body and escaped to the ceiling. As I hung on to a light, I heard my own voice answer the question easily and calmly. Another question, another sane answer. It was going to be all right. I came back into my body, turned a bit in my swivel chair and kicked off my shoes. I no longer noticed the cameras and bright lights. This was just a casual conversation.

The taping was over very quickly. The crew closed in to take our mics off. Someone ate the cheeseburger. Kent complimented me on my fresh approach and candid manner. I chastised him for not following the script and then thanked him for it, for putting me totally at ease. It was a great beginning for both of us. We made a good team!

At last my creativity had a platform. In addition to my TV appearances, I developed recipes, wrote news releases and recorded brief public service announcements for radio stations. It was a goal of mine to make personal contact with every newspaper and radio station in our territory, Eastern Massachusetts, and I took one afternoon each week for that purpose. Sitting at a desk for too long made me restless. Meandering around the New England countryside was more my style.

My fear of public speaking diminished as I gained experience. Eventually I even enjoyed the food demonstrations I gave before live audiences, the press parties I hosted and the dairy industry meetings I spoke at. I had come a long way from my school days when I blushed every time I was called on. Even so, it took a few months before I felt confident enough to tell my friends to watch me on TV. During my tapings I was certain my speaking was choppy and ineffective, but later, watching the show, I was amazed at how effective I actually was. I had to continually remind myself the person I was watching was me! It was a relief to know there was a big discrepancy between how I felt inside and how I appeared to others. The many fan letters I received after each appearance helped reassure me this was true.

My relationship with Kent also boosted my confidence immensely. He continually praised my performance, saying I had natural ability and good taste, and that he trusted my judgment implicitly. After each TV taping, we also taped a radio show. The two performances made us both so emotionally high that we couldn't think of going back to our offices. Instead, we lunched together and spent a few hours unwinding. Kent's sense of humor sparked mine, so I fully enjoyed myself. Rarely did I make it back to the Dairy Council before quitting time. After my co-workers left, I remained to wash the dishes from my TV preparations and to come back to earth with no one else around.

I never viewed my relationship with Kent as anything but purely professional. He was married and I was very much in love with Jack. Even with increasing invitations to join him for various press functions, I remained oblivious to what was happening. Only when I turned down an invitation to join him for a big hotel opening and he sent me a dozen red roses with a note begging me to accompany him, did I realize he had other ideas about our relationship! He asked me to marry him. When I pointed out that he was already married, he said if I would say "yes" he would get divorced. I told him to get divorced first, then ask me. (I was learning!) As I suspected, he didn't want to chance it. We left it at this impasse and continued to enjoy each other's company professionally—except when he persisted his case, when we were alone in an elevator, or suddenly in the middle of a totally unrelated conversation. Once he even followed me down Storrow Drive in Boston honking and yelling "marry me!" out his window. In retrospect, I realized this was the older man the astrologer had referred to, who would ask me to marry him and that I wouldn't.

Jack and I continued our weekend rendezvous in New Haven and in Boston. I had changed a great deal since our first meeting only nine months before. Somehow, Jack's validation of who I was propelled me to live in a truer, fuller self. His lack of passing judgment and his insistence I speak and act exactly as I felt helped alleviate my fear of not being accepted. A barrier removed, I was more "real," closer to the world. I had released the limited view I held of myself in order to grow into the expanded image Jack reflected. The tip of the iceberg was melting, allowing a whole new surface, a greater part of myself, to emerge.

I experienced complete peace when Jack and I were together. The only real glitch in our relationship was his "other life," his wife and children. Increasingly, Jack tried to merge his two lives, talking about how wonderful it would be if all of us lived together. He speculated on how his wife, Karen, and I would get along, and imagined our meeting. The frustration of not being able to unite the two parts of himself took its toll. Jack began experiencing severe pains in this heart. His doctor warned him to end whatever was creating his stress, otherwise, he was headed for a heart attack.

I didn't know how to help. Not seeing each other again certainly wasn't the answer. I began dreaming of Karen, that we met in a department store and became instant friends. Every night for a week my dreams were different versions of our meeting and getting to know each other. Though I had never seen a picture of Karen, I was sure I would recognize her. At the end of the week, Jack instructed me not to come to New Haven as planned. He would be tied up at work most of the weekend. Not that I didn't believe him, but I sensed something was wrong. After work on Friday, I headed to New Haven as usual.

When I called Jack to tell him I was there, he didn't seem surprised, angry or pleased. He said he would be right over. When he arrived he was very quiet and looked exhausted. Something in his manner kept me from asking what was going on. He bought me a hamburger and said he had already eaten. I could still feel our love and closeness, but something had changed. Jack didn't give me any clues until I finished eating. Then he asked why I had come. I told him I wasn't sure except I felt I was supposed to be there. I told him of my dreams about Karen. He verified my descriptions of her and said she wanted to meet me. *Wanted to meet me?* She knew about me!

Jack had been careless and Karen had confronted him about her suspicions. They had spent the week sorting through what our relationship meant to their marriage. They still weren't sure how it fit in, but they did know that they loved each other and wanted to stay together. When Karen found out I was in New Haven, she wanted to meet me that evening.

A bomb hit! I went limp with the onslaught of conflicting emotions. I couldn't handle meeting Karen right then. Instead, Jack would have her call me in the next couple of weeks to arrange a time I could visit. Jack assured me he loved me as much as ever and everything would work out.

Back in Boston I recovered from the shock of the weekend's events, and grew more curious about meeting Karen. The day Martin Luther King was assassinated, Jack called to express his concern about the rioting in Boston and insisted I stay home from work that day. Even from a distance he was monitoring my safety! I assured him I would comply with his wishes. Shortly after his call, the phone rang again. It was Karen. Jack had instructed her to stay home, also! We had instant empathy and talked like old friends. When Karen invited me to visit the next weekend, I agreed and insisted I stay at the hotel rather than with the family.

When I checked in at the Sheraton desk the next weekend, I was informed the rooms were overbooked due to a big convention. My usual room couldn't be saved for me. There was nothing available at any of the other hotels in town, either. "That settles it," Jack said when he came to pick me up, "you will stay with us!" Protesting at first, but unable to suggest an alternative, I reluctantly let Jack and his two-year old son, who eyed me suspiciously, drive me to their home.

Karen greeted me amiably and introduced me to the three children who waited to meet their mother's "old college friend." After a few moments of awkward small talk, the usual big-family activity resumed, and Jack, Karen and I settled comfortably in the living room to drink coffee and talk. It felt amazingly normal for the three of us to be together. Even when Jack went to take a nap, I felt perfectly at ease with Karen. Later, when Karen and Jack left to go on an errand, I stayed home with the children, providing piggyback rides and supervising games in the back yard.

After dinner, when the children had been tucked into bed, Karen, Jack and I lounged on the living room floor and enjoyed each other's company into the wee hours. It was all very cozy and congenial—until bedtime. Then Jack and Karen each hugged me goodnight before going up the stairs together. Reality struck! Though intellectually I knew Jack could never fully be with me, I needed this experience to make it a truth for me. I was left to sleep on the couch. I fidgeted and cried intermittently all night.

Jack came down early in the morning and held me in his arms. He had been well aware of my dilemma and, like me, didn't get much sleep. We talked with our usual intimacy and assured each other of our love. Neither of us had any insights as to where all of this was going. To keep our emotions at bay, we busied ourselves with making Sunday morning pancakes for the family. The day proceeded much as the one before it, with us enjoying each other's company and the family activities. When it was time for me to leave, I received four wonderful hugs from the kids, even the littlest, who by then had become my best buddy. Before Jack took me to the train, Karen and I had a few minutes alone in the kitchen together to say good-by—truly we were old friends.

For weeks I struggled with my emotions and conflicting thoughts. Jack wanted to buy a house for me in New Haven. He still had the notion we could all live an integrated life together. When he came to visit me in Boston, I thought about Karen in New Haven. I didn't want to take Jack away from her or his family. Maybe living together in harmony was possible. Jack was my other half, he made me feel whole. I didn't want to live without that complete-ness. Yet, the knowing that I had some greater pur-pose to accomplish in life was growing stronger. If I were to settle for living to be with Jack, I would never fulfill my purpose. The completeness I felt with him would keep me from desiring anything else. I wouldn't have the motivation to go out into the world and do what I needed to do. The meaning of the astrologer's words became clear. I must pull myself out of the relationship.

My decision made, I called Jack at work. "Are you going to marry me?" I asked.

Surprised, he stuttered, "Well, no, of course not, you know. . . oh, I see what you are doing. " His voice became very quiet. "This is it, isn't it? You've called to say good-by."

I assured him we didn't have to cut off the relationship altogether. We could still talk on the phone and write, but we did need to stop seeing each other. I told him I loved him and hung up the phone. I was numb, completely nonfunctional. Once again, I felt as if someone close to me had just died, the same way I felt when Jack and I tried to stay apart before. This time, however, I knew I would have to live it out . . . I couldn't give in. It would take all the strength I had.

I went through the motions of living without feeling joy or sadness. I simply existed. Occasionally Jack and I talked on the phone, but even he seemed on a distant pole of my frozen heart. I got up, went to work, came home and went to bed. Little in life interested me. Sometimes I tried going out with friends or to the ocean, but it was more effort than it was worth. I had little desire for anything but sleep.

Sally, the woman in the apartment across the hall, was concerned about me. She decided I needed to meet a new man. After much nagging, she finally convinced me to accompany her to one of her favorite night spots. I consented only because I thought the distraction might be good for me. I had no interest in meeting men.

As soon as we arrived at the club, Sally instantly began flaunting her colors. This usually drab matron set about weaving a man-catching web around our table. I couldn't believe her methods! She batted her eyes conspicuously at any passing potentials. Even more unbelievable was the fact her methods worked! Men, very attractive men, were lured in like flies. Sally mesmerized them with her soothing voice while she inspected them unmercifully. If they wore a wedding ring, she told them bluntly to leave. She didn't want to waste any time. If they passed the appearance test, she probed for indications of wealth and prestige. It didn't take long for me to realize she wasn't looking for a man for me. It was each woman for herself. The motivation not being there for me, I contented myself to watching her. The witnessing of such blatant prowess in husband-hunting shocked me out of my lethargy. I had to smile!

Though I declined Sally's ensuing invitations for evening outings, I was grateful for her stoking some life into me. I wrote a letter to my cousin Nancy in Turkey, who was ending her two-year stint with the Peace Corps, and asked her to come to Boston to live with me. She promptly accepted my offer.

When Nancy arrived, we discovered we were suffering similar maladies. The man she had been involved with in the Peace Corps had deserted her for an old love. Being in the same "frame of heart," we traipsed off together, discovering new beaches where we could lay in the sun and heal ourselves.

Youri

Gradually, I adjusted to Jack's absence in my life. Just knowing he existed made me happy. I began to socialize more frequently, but still had no desire to meet other men.

At work, a public relations consultant came to help me with a special promotion. She was a creative spark plug who enlivened the office with crazy antics, and a hilarious sense of humor. When she invited Nancy and myself to her home for dinner one weekend, I anticipated a thoroughly entertaining evening. Little was I prepared for what evolved.

Over a delicious meal, the conversation took a curious bent. We began discussing unusual occurrences in our lives. I described the strange phenomena Jack and I experienced together, and another guest related her adventures with a ouija board. Since neither Nancy nor I knew anything about ouija boards, our hostess agreed to show us one. She went out of the room and returned with a box. In it appeared to be some kind of game board with the alphabet and numbers on it. There was a separate piece, a much smaller, pointed board on legs, that you were to put on the larger board and touch lightly with your finger tips without exerting pressure. The idea was to ask a question and then wait for the piece to move on its own to the letters on the board, spelling out an answer that was supposedly a communication from an unseen entity or spirit, often a deceased relative. Nancy and I looked at each other with raised eyebrows. We were willing to try.

Four of us placed our fingers on the small platform and someone asked a question. Almost immediately the pointer began to move. Letter to letter, a reply was spelled out. I was amazed and skeptical. Certainly someone was directing the piece somehow. As we continued, the spelling suddenly changed into something that we couldn't understand. A foreign language, perhaps? Laboriously the pointer moved in response to our demands for clarity. Finally, we could make out the meaning. It instructed Nancy and myself to be the only ones on the board. When we complied, the movements became very distinct and the words clear. "I am Caroline, your grandmother." Indeed, our fathers' mother who had died before we were born was named Caroline! We were both unnerved. Neither of us knew much about our grandmother nor had we ever mentioned her to each other. When we attempted to get more information from the board, nothing happened. Apparently, our grandmother just wanted to say hello. Fascinated, we borrowed the board from our hostess when we left for home that evening.

Try as we might over the next several days, no other messages came through when we worked the ouija board by ourselves. We decided that someone at the dinner party must have been a good "receiver" and had acted as a kind of grounding force for us. When I called Jack to ask if he knew how the ouija board worked, he didn't, but was so intrigued by our experience he bought a board for himself and spent many hours experimenting with it. His results were not much better than ours had been.

At a press party the next weekend, a new acquaintance asked if I wanted to leave and go dancing somewhere. I agreed and soon we were in the car and on our way. Suddenly, I looked at my companion and said, "I have to go home! I'm going to get a phone call. Please hurry!" My startled date thought I was kidding and began teasing me as he continued driving toward our original destination. When I became frantic, he realized I was serious and turned the car around. Arriving at the apartment building, I flew out of the car and up the stairs, my date at my heels. As I opened the door, we could hear the phone ringing. I quickly apologized, said good-by, and ran to answer the phone.

It was Jack calling to tell me about the breakthrough he and Karen had on the ouija board. An entity, calling itself a "guide," was clearly spelling messages to them. Jack excitedly related the details, but I felt somewhat giddy after having a drink or two at the press party and couldn't take him seriously. Jokingly, I told him to ask his guide if I had a guide.

Hanging up the phone, I suddenly felt very strange. There was an odd pressure on my head, as if someone were pushing on me from above, and a tingling sensation throughout my body. Compulsively, I searched the apartment for a pen and some paper and frantically sought a comfortable place to sit. Nothing felt right until I sat on the bathroom floor next to the electric heater. With the paper in front of me on the floor, I held the pencil posed to write. For a second I wondered why I was doing this. What was going on? Then, my hand began moving . . . but *I* wasn't moving it! It was propelled by its own volition, without any guidance from me. Something appeared on the paper: *IloveyouIloveyouIloveyou.* All the words flowed together without spaces between. I laughed. This must be Jack! Some more of our magic. "I love you, too," I said out loud.

ILOVEYOU, the pencil continued to write in bigger and bigger letters pushing down harder, almost tearing the paper.

A warmth radiated from somewhere to the right of me. Someone, it seemed, was standing next to me. "Who are you?" I asked, feeling very, very happy— joyful!

IamYourIloveyouIloveyouIloveyou!
Astonished, I asked, "What are you?"
IamaboyYouareagirl.

"I *know* that! But *what* are you?" I asked impatiently.

Iamaguide.

A door opened in the next room. . . . Nancy was home. The "spell" was broken. I quickly gathered up the writings and flung them under my bed. I greeted my cousin without mentioning what had just happened. I didn't *know* what had just happened! I needed time to think and assimilate the experience without talking about it, even to Jack.

In the next few weeks I tried sitting quietly with a pencil and paper, hoping to repeat the experience with Youri. Nothing happened until one night when I was at the office alone, writing at my desk. I was half-conscious of a strong pressure on my head, but being intent on finishing what I was doing and going home, I continued my work. The pressure increased and I instinctively rubbed the top of my head with one hand as I wrote with the other. Suddenly, I realized how awful I felt—very depressed, as if I would cry at any moment.

Something released inside me and the pen in my hand took on a life of its own, pulling my hand with it, *Iloveyou Iloveyou!* Youri joyfully repeated, *Iloveyou Iloveyou Iloveyou Iamaguide.*

Frantically, I tried to get him to say more. "What is a guide? Why have you come? Why do you call yourself Youri?" But he wouldn't answer.

Bob

After taping my monthly TV show in New Bedford in southern Massachusetts, I usually gave Diane, the local hostess for the children's show, Romper Room, a ride home. She lived in Winthrop, a little town on the ocean just outside of Boston, not far out of my way. As we drove, Diane often told me stories about her brother, Bob, who had recently completed his master's degree in composition at the Boston Conservatory and was a talented clarinetist. He was currently playing music in New York and waiting word from the draft board. They both hoped he wouldn't be inducted and sent to the war in Vietnam. Diane was convinced he and I were very much alike— even in the way we sneezed. "You have to meet him sometime when he comes home from New York," she told me. "You would like each other."

Diane usually ate dinner with her parents at their house before going to her own home, and always invited me to join her. Usually, I was too wound up after my show in New Bedford and wanted to hurry home to relax and come back to earth by myself, but one night Diane insisted so emphatically I finally accepted the invitation.

As soon as I walked into the house I realized why Diane had been so insistent—Bob was home! When we were introduced, Bob said Diane had told him all about me, and that I was much prettier than he expected. While we enjoyed a lively dinner, everyone talking at once, Bob and I eyed each other curiously and smiled frequently. He was not at all what I expected, not at all like Diane. I liked his twinkling eyes and his fresh enthusiasm for life. He was constantly joking and laughing and getting up from his chair to show me something. After dinner, he whisked me into the living room to hear the record he had just made. It was avant-garde jazz and I liked it. It was much more exciting than the traditional jazz I had often gone to hear in Philadelphia. Bob was so pleased with my enthusiasm, he invited me to go for a ride—in *my* new Volvo!

We drove up the north shore along the ocean, talking easily on many subjects. After a half-hour, we parked the car and walked to the water. Bob took my hand to guide me over the large rocks until we found a dry place to sit. We watched the crashing surf and pointed to the stars and constellations we recognized. The next thing I knew, Bob was kissing me!

He invited me out to dinner the next night, and the next and the next. We were together as much as possible in the next two weeks. Diane was right—we *were* very much alike! But we didn't sneeze the same, as she said, nor were our similarities obvious. In fact, to all appearances we were very different. Bob looked the part of a struggling musician, dressed in turtleneck and jeans, living in a "pad," still dependent on his parents for support. He was an outspoken Easterner, often stirring up controversy. I was the successful career woman living independently, very conscientious about my responsibilities, a mild-mannered Midwesterner who avoided conflict. Where we hit the common cord was on the inside. We were each searching for our spiritual purpose, aware of levels of being other than the physical. It didn't take long for us to each confess, " If I were to get married now, I would marry you!"

Bob received notice to report for military duty on the Wednesday before Thanksgiving. He hoped to be granted a medical deferment for his bad back but wouldn't know until after he reported and was given a physical exam. Bob's folks invited me to a family send-off for him, an early Thanksgiving dinner.

On Wednesday, Bob reported to the draft board carrying his toothbrush and other personal items in a bag. His family and I held our breath. It was hard to imagine Bob fighting in a war, and to think of his career preempted after all those years of preparation. Now, too, there was our relationship just beginning.

I tried to focus on preparations for the Thanksgiving feast I would cook for friends the next day.

Around five o'clock that evening, the phone rang. It was Bob! His bad back had won him a reprieve! He was coming right over. We joyously danced down the supermarket aisles that night grabbing last minute items for the *real* Thanksgiving we would celebrate.

Bob and I took turns visiting each other either in New York or in Boston, spending as much time together as we could. One night when Bob was in Boston and driving me home after an evening together, my thoughts suddenly turned to Jack. A wave of depression hit with such impact I almost cried out. Tears welled up in my eyes. What was going on? Only moments before I was feeling very much in love and very happy. A strong pressure pushed down on my head. I tried not to panic. Then it dawned on me— Youri was wanting to come through! As soon as we were in the apartment I ran to get some paper and a pen. When Bob went to do something in another room, I invited Youri to write through me.

Get away from Bob! he scribbled quickly.

I was stunned, and afraid. I yelled for Bob. When he came running, I quickly explained what had just happened. "Oh, automatic writing," he said calmly. "Just ask Youri why you should get away from me."

Putting aside my surprise at Bob's knowledge and placidity about what was going on, I once again put pen to paper. Silently, I asked Youri to explain his command. The pen took off in a flurry of fast circles and meaningless scrawls. Maybe I needed to be alone with Youri, Bob suggested. Once Bob left the room, Youri settled down and wrote legibly. He explained: He had been a husband of mine in Russia in a previous lifetime. He loved me so much he wanted to continue to be with me while I was incarnated and he wasn't. He chose to be a guide for me to help in whatever ways he could. Bob had been his handsome cousin—who was also attracted to me. Now that Bob was with me in the flesh, Youri was jealous!

Reincarnation was not a philosophy I could embrace easily. Years before I had considered it briefly as an Eastern philosophy and then discarded it as not being plausible, at least not as I understoond it—that after death you could be reborn as a human, or an animal. This never "felt right" or made sense to me and I never explored the concept further. I developed my own philosophy, that we were in this life to learn something and that each person evolved to a certain psychological state before being ready to die. This state could come at any age. The reason for needing to do this was a puzzle, but this was as far as I had gotten in explaining the why of existence.

I could accept Youri as long as I thought of him as some kind of entity "out there" somewhere. But now he was telling me he was the same kind of being as I was, having been incarnate, and that I lived as some other person before! My already boggled mind was sledgehammered, activating anew all my unanswered questions about the nature of existence.

Bob and I talked all that night. He told me about his teacher who introduced him to metaphysics and taught him how to meditate. Automatic writing was something he had heard about but never tried. He also knew about the existence of guides, but didn't understand the nature of their being anymore than I did.

During the next few weeks, Bob and I spent many hours "talking" to Youri. He accepted that Bob had "honorable" intentions towards me and willingly answered his questions, as well as mine. When we asked him about reincarnation, he said Earth is a schoolhouse that we keep returning to. We move up grades as we learn our lessons, lifetime after lifetime, until we "graduate" and no longer need to come back again. When we asked about the nature of guides, he informed us that guides are entities the same as we are, but that instead of being incarnated, they remain in spirit form. They further their knowledge by learning from the experience of the incarnated individuals they assist.

Everyone has an "inner guide," sometimes referred to as a "guardian angel," who remains with the person from birth to death. This special relationship between a guide and an incarnated individual is agreed to beforehand (before birth) and is symbiotic; each contributes to the other's learning. The main function of the inner guide is to help the incarnated connect with their own "higher" self (that part of consciousness that is the connection of each person to the rest of the universe), and to assist them in attaining self fulfillment. There are guides other than inner guides, also. These "activities guides" are called forth by the higher self to assist in all areas of human endeavor from childbirth, healing, creating, to dying. Most people are not in conscious communication with their guides, or even aware that they exist. Awareness is not important, but, as I was to find out, very helpful.

According to Youri, guides take on a "personality" that can best communicate what is needed to the person being helped. Youri was a playful, emotional persona, frequently assuring me of his love. I was fascinated by the ramifications of reincarnation and endlessly asked him about my connections with family and friends. He patiently answered all my questions.

On the other hand, Bob's guide demanded that Bob work, work, WORK! From the first moment the two had a joyful meeting through automatic writing, they "talked" constantly. Bob was instructed to get busy and compose several specified pieces. Heaven forbid if Bob asked his guide to repeat or further explain something! The guide bore down very heavily on the pen, making sure his message got through.

One day when we were visiting his folks, Bob asked me if I wanted to help his father. He was suffering a kidney stone attack and was in great pain. When we visited Dr. Fritz in his bedroom, he told us that if the stone didn't pass during the night, he would have to be operated on the next day. After leaving the bedroom, Bob led me down to the family room in the basement. We sat with our eyes closed while Bob said a protection prayer, asking for only that which was "good and needful." We then imagined rays of white light filling our bodies and moving out through the palms of our hands. Immediately, I felt a warm sensation flow though me, with a concentration of heat in my hands. In my mind I visualized light flowing to Dr. Fritz. After a few intense minutes of my hands throbbing and my whole being seemingly pulled toward Bob's father, we both "saw" that he would pass the stone, and "felt" the pain being relieved. The tension was released and we opened our eyes.

We immediately ran up the two flights of stairs to Dr. Fritz's bedroom and asked how he was feeling. He said it was amazing, he all of a sudden was feeling so much better, and all of his pain was gone. Bob and I smiled at each other. Dr. Fritz had no idea of what we had done and would have pooh-poohed it if he had known, calling it all a coincidence. He passed the stone that night.

Newlyweds

In February 1969, three months after we met, Bob and I announced we would be married the following September. We wanted to have a sunrise wedding somewhere on a cliff overlooking the ocean and exchange vows we would write ourselves. To avoid any religious overtone (Bob's family was Jewish and mine Protestant), we planned to ask a justice of the peace to marry us. While Bob was busy in New York, it would be my task to find the right location for the ceremony. A vague memory of a little park overlooking the ocean that Nancy and I discovered on one of our excursions came to mind. It would be the perfect place. I set out to search for it in the area around Marblehead, an old fishing village on the north shore above Boston.

After many days of systematically exploring likely streets leading to the ocean, I still couldn't locate the park I remembered. Frustrated, I tried asking some of the local residents for ideas. I knew the park was close, but with all the little winding streets I kept getting lost in the maze—coming to dead ends or finding myself going past the same spots again and again. Then someone suggested I investigate the Marblehead lighthouse.

This had to be it, I thought as I drove out the winding road to the peninsula. But when I jumped out of the car and looked around, my heart sank. It was a beautiful spot, but it didn't match the images that persisted in my memory. Discouraged, I took a deep breath and sat down. I had no idea where to look next. I took some sand in my hand and let it run soothingly out through my fingers while my eyes drank in the tranquility of the seascape. Suddenly, I jumped to my feet and peered across the bay to the opposite shore. *There it was!*

Asking the first person I could find what the place was called, I followed the directions I was given to Fort Sewall. It was as my memory recalled: a perfect place for our wedding. The park topped a high rocky embankment that jutted out into the ocean. A sidewalk circled the perimeter of a large grassy area where red-bricked remnants of a historic fort were visible. I found the ideal place for our ceremony on a large flat rock, on the northernmost point of the cliff overlooking the open sea. The surf pounding at the base would provide our music. I could hardly wait to show Bob!

That weekend when Bob came up from New York, I led him with great mystery to Fort Sewall.

"This is it!" I said triumphantly when we got out of the car.

Bob stared at me in amazement, "Ellen, don't you recognize this place?"

"Well, yes," I said, "It's where Nancy and I ended up one day when we were lost."

"And," he exclaimed excitedly, "this is where I took you the first night we met!"

Then, as I looked around, I could see—the same rocks, of course! It had been dark that night and, besides, who was paying attention to the landscape?

My next step was to ask permission from the town fathers to use Fort Sewall for the wedding. This was much easier said than done! In this traditional, conservative New England town, the idea of getting married on a rocky cliff at dawn was considered weird, and the fact we wanted to write our own ceremony to be officiated over by the town clerk, the Justice of the Peace, made us suspect. Certainly we must be "hippies," undesirables who would rock the cherished tranquility of this sleepy town. Our request for the use of the park was immediately put on hold by the Board of Selectmen. They would discuss the issue at the next monthly meeting and get back to us.

The idea of waiting another month to finalize the location for our wedding made me nervous, but I was so certain that Fort Sewall was Our Spot I went ahead with our plans and made an appointment with Marblehead's Justice of the Peace, Betty Brown. Bob and I wore our most conservative clothes for the meeting. After listening to our plans for a sunrise ceremony, Mrs. Brown made it quite clear that the only reason she would agree to marry us was the oath she took as Justice of the Peace requiring her to marry anyone who requested it. We didn't dare tell her right then the rest of our plan—to have two ceremonies—one at dawn for us and our immediate families, and then another later in the day for Bob's grandmother, who wouldn't be able to make the earlier time, and for all our other relatives and friends.

A month later, I received a call from a Mr. Jordan, one of the selectmen. Thinking the hesitations of his fellows were unjustified, he offered help to push our request through. He suggested I write a letter to the board and include the details for our wedding arrangements and the specific reasons we wanted our ceremony to take place on the ocean at sunrise. I immediately complied, and soon after received a happy call from Mr. Jordan reporting that our request was granted. Mr. Jordan's sincere compassion and warmth touched my heart. I felt very connected to this man who saw his role in life as the champion for the underdog.

When a friend and I spent a day in Marblehead searching for the right location for a second marriage ceremony and our reception, we checked out several unsuitable places before taking a break for lunch. We drove to a small pub, locally famous for their seafood, and joined the long line of people waiting to get in. Striking up a conversation with the people in front of us, I asked if they had any suggestions for a place for a wedding reception. They politely asked when the wedding would be. When I told them, the light of recognition beamed forth. "*You* are the kook who is getting married at Fort Sewall at dawn!"

I was stunned. *How did these people know about my wedding?* I nodded my head and they explained: They had read the notice in the paper—all actions by the selectmen were routinely published. Fortunately, these Marbleheadians thought our plans were wonderful and, in fact, seemed to admire my spirit. Soon we were gabbing away like old friends. I told them the whole story about finding Fort Sewell and the trouble we had in getting sanction from the Board of Selectmen. When I mentioned Mr. Jordan and how grateful I was to him, they said he was a good friend of theirs and that he would probably be along any minute.

Inside the restaurant we crowded together in a booth while one of our newfound friends went to the bar to get us drinks. Before long there was a steady stream of onlookers gawking curiously at me. Apparently our drink-bringer had used the opportunity to tell everyone he could that he had met the kook mentioned in the paper!

I was just finishing up my clam chowder when I sensed a commotion at the door. Suddenly an elfish, gray-haired gentleman stood in front of the table. Mr. Jordan! We needed no introduction and immediately embraced. My new friends looked at us understandingly and excused themselves, saying they had to leave. Mr. Jordan sat down and put his hand over mine on the table. Instant love! I expressed my gratitude to him and decreed he must come to the wedding. He said he wouldn't miss it! Indeed he didn't, and fortunately for me he was the first one there.

On the morning of the wedding everything was dark at five thirty in the morning, and the maze of Marblehead streets looked very different. Dressed in my wedding gown, I drove with my sister, my maid of honor, toward Ft. Sewall. Nothing looked familiar and soon I was lost! When another car turned onto the empty street in front of me, I instinctively followed it. In a few minutes we arrived safely at Fort Sewall. Mr. Jordan stepped out of the other car, and, again, I embraced him in gratitude.

When Bob and I arrived back in Boston after our two-week honeymoon in Canada, we discovered we were quite the celebrities. We were amazed to find the story of our sunrise wedding had been carried by newspapers around the country, and that the *Marblehead Messenger* had written an editorial. "Will Saturday morning's sunrise wedding at Fort Sewall touch off a trend?" After such a magical start to our union, Bob and I settled into the apartment Bob had found for us in Nyack, New York. It was a classic newlywed's first abode—adequate but small, with a quaint bathroom in the hall outside the apartment. We were just half an hour from New York over the Tappen Zee Bridge, and yet, within minutes of the woods.

To savor the first months together as husband and wife, we extended our honeymoon by living off the money we had received as wedding gifts. I had quit my job at the Dairy Council and Bob's band only played occasional gigs that paid anything. We spent our days walking in the woods, playing tennis, exploring country roads, watching television, and cooking elaborate meals together. We decorated our apartment with artwork we created and produced an abundance of wire sculptures and earrings we eventually gave away as gifts or sold to friends.

When our finances inevitably dwindled, I worked as an office temporary, choosing jobs and work times that best afforded our continued relaxed lifestyle. Bob concentrated on his composing and rehearsed with his rock band in New York.

This initial time in our marriage was important not only for establishing a well-rounded relationship with each other, but also for the opportunity it provided to focus on our connection with the guides. When the guides explained that meditation was the key to opening our channels to them and to our higher selves, and the way to consciously tap the pool of universal knowing, we meditated daily. This, however, wasn't easy for me. My mind was constantly occupied with planning in great detail what I wanted to accomplish the rest of the day. I had a hard time focusing. When I tried blocking my thoughts, I stopped breathing as well! The guides suggested I drink a little beer or wine first or soak in the bathtub to help relax. The beer helped to slow my mind, but soaking in the bathtub made me more tense. I was afraid I would fall asleep and drown! The guides assured me they would wake me up before that could happen. They also suggested I keep my mind from wandering by imagining a cross of white light. The light would get brighter and brighter until it totally encompassed me with warmth and melted my thoughts away. Gradually, I experienced moments of mental quiet.

After meditating, Bob and I individually asked questions of our guides and received the answers through automatic writing. In one of these sessions my conversation with Youri led me to questioning whether or not, indeed, he was my "inner" guide. Up to this point I had assumed he was, but when I asked point blank, he answered in a very little voice—in tiny, barely visible writing—that he wasn't. I felt betrayed! Why hadn't he told me? He replied that he was afraid that if I knew who my inner guide was, I wouldn't want to talk to him again. "Oh, Youri," I told him out loud, "of course I would still want to talk to you! I love you!" Apparently convinced, he then informed me my inner guide's name was Allen.

Allen had a whole different feel to him. He was very polite and reassuring. He told me he was Japanese and drew his picture—a wonderful line drawing of himself meditating. He immediately informed me we had work to do together, that he wanted to instruct me about the importance of environment so I could write a series of articles on the subject.

Talking to Allen was tiring. I could only concentrate for a short time before feeling sleepy. Part of the problem, Allen explained, was that I was too "open." I received subtle vibrations easily and, therefore, was sensitive to anything around me. I wasn't discriminating about what I allowed "in." He had me concentrate on his vibration, consciously choosing to allow only him to write through me. Too often when I gave over the control of my hand to Allen, the pen would get "snatched" by another entity and a battle would ensue. Incomplete sentences and mixed thoughts would result. The switching of the different energies exhausted me. I had to be firm and allow only Allen to come through by declaring my intention very "loudly," that I would respond to Allen only, no one else. If I felt the energy in my hand switching, I stopped immediately and refused to write. When I felt Allen come back, I allowed him access to my hand again.

One of the ways I could recognize when Allen was with me was a sign he gave me, a horizontal, elongated eight, the sign for infinity. Whenever Allen was present, the pen would make the sign very strongly and I could "feel" it was Allen. If the energy began to switch, I controlled the pen and focused on the infinity sign until the pen began drawing it without my help.

To become more sensitive to Allen, I played tic-tac-toe with him. I wrote my "X's" and then let go of

control in my hand to feel where Allen wanted his
"O's." His higher perspective gave him the edge—he
won more often than I did! When we played hang-
man together, he picked a word and indicated
through my hand how many blank spaces, one for
each letter in the word, I needed to fill. I had to guess
by process of elimination what the letters were. Again,
it wasn't fair. His vocabulary was bigger than mine!

When Bob and I individually felt confident
enough in our communication with our guides, we
began having sessions together in which one of us
asked a question and the other wrote the answer via
the guides. We found that we could "speak" to each
other's guide interchangeably. This was especially
helpful with personal issues that we were emotional
about. Having the other person channel our guide
gave a distance and helped us to be more receptive
to the advice. It also helped us trust the information
we received about ourselves. Often the replies to our
inquiries were so positive we were sure we were sub-
consciously making up what we wished were true.

In fact, at times the whole concept of guides and
our experience of what was happening to us seemed
so weird and inconceivable that we had extreme
doubts about whether any of it was real. No one else
we knew had experienced what we were, and there
were few books on the subject. We often wondered if
we were making it all up. One way we tested ourselves was to ask a question neither of us knew the
answer to and then go into different rooms to receive

replies from our individual guides. The answers always jibed. It was when we began to ask for advice and predictions about our future that our doubts really set in.

At first we asked short term questions that we would soon know the answers to. About Bob's band, we asked whether the recording offers the group received would pan out. We were told "yes," but the truth was, they didn't. After too many times of getting our hopes up, we were disgusted and decided to go on strike. We didn't talk to the guides for a week! Then we called a pow-wow and asked our spirit friends why their predictions weren't happening and why their timing was off.

Their explanation was that our channels needed to be strengthened, both from their side and from ours, that it takes practice to maneuver the different planes of consciousness. Timing, they said, was the hardest thing to predict. On their level, time didn't exist. They were learning how to adjust to our time perception. Of course, too, they quickly stressed, they were not infallible, that they were "people," too, and could only guide us from their level of awareness. Ultimately, we needed to trust ourselves and make decisions based on our own knowing, not theirs. They were there to lead us to a greater part of ourselves and to teach us to trust our own knowing.

With this explanation, we relaxed and learned to compare our spirit friends' information with our own innate knowing to see if it felt right. We found most of the information we received from our guides was indeed very helpful, especially about the truly important issues. It was only with more trivial matters that we found discrepancies. Our guides were back in our good graces and our confrontation with them helped us develop a closer feeling of "family. " We cracked jokes with our guides and had fun, affectionate and humorous conversations with them. They, in turn, loved amusing us with "people stories," their version of our "ghost stories!"

When doubts about our perception of the guides persisted, the guides came through with more dramatic evidence that they, indeed, did exist, and that they were entities separate from us. One morning Bob and I went ice skating on one of our favorite lakes. At noon we took off our skates and hiked up in the cliffs surrounding the lake to find a spot to eat our lunch. I wanted to find a place with a view and climbed higher up the rocks. Bob stayed lower and went ahead of me. As I pulled myself up onto a ledge I bumped my head hard against a steel beam jutting out from above. For a moment I was so stunned, I sat down and let my head spin. After a bit, Bob called to me asking where I was. I said I would be right down and never mentioned the incident to him. At home that night I was in the kitchen washing the dishes. Feeling very tired and a little nauseous, I decided my monthly period must be starting. Bob called from the bedroom saying Allen wanted to talk to me. I answered back that I was too tired and didn't want to talk to him. I was feeling a little guilty about not focusing on the environmental articles Allen wanted me to write. I was not in the mood to be reprimanded. The next thing I knew, Bob was in the kitchen taking my hand and pulling me into the bedroom. "You *have* to write to Allen!" he said.

Bob handed me a pen and pad of paper and I let my hand relax. *You must go to the hospital!* Allen wrote. *You have a brain concussion.* Bob was looking over my shoulder. "That's what I was getting!" he said. "It just didn't make sense but I couldn't get the thought out of my mind." I explained how I had hit my head that day.

Bob rushed me out the door and to the emergency room of the local hospital. Indeed, I had a brain concussion and was hemorrhaging. The doctor said it was serious but not critical. It was important to stay in bed and rest, not be up running around. Bob would need to keep a close watch on me.

I stayed in bed and slept most of the next week. Every once in a while, I woke up with the thought that I needed to shift my position. The guides explained I needed to be careful of blood clotting. They were monitoring my progress and let me know when I needed to move or drink more liquids.

Certainly, this experience had given us proof without a doubt that the guides existed outside ourselves and that their information could be trusted. Being human, however, we seemed to need drama on a continual basis to hold our trust. One day when I was sitting in the quiet of the bathroom playing tic-tac-toe with Allen, I began to feel light-headed and emotional. Allen began to write, *go to Bob, go to Bob.* Overwhelmed by anxiety, I ran into the apartment and found Bob in the bedroom. Sobbing hysterically, I didn't make much sense. I attempted to explain that my mind felt as if it would burst, and as if something was trying to take it over. Bob recited the Lord's Prayer and instructed me to do likewise. I couldn't focus. When Bob asked the guides what was going on, they told us that I was having union of mind with a friend of ours from Boston who occasionally had psychotic spells.

Sensing the inner struggle he experienced, I had previously offered myself in meditation to be a spiritual vehicle for our friend's healing. I calmed down and began "seeing" with Bob what his situation was. We saw him with a woman friend in an isolated cabin in the Vermont woods. Although we were in frequent communication with these friends, neither of them had mentioned that they might go to Vermont. We saw our friend hitting his head against the wall while our woman friend tried to hold him back and have him sit down. We "sent" the strong message, *call us ,* to her. We "heard" back: *I can't. There is no telephone here and I don't want to leave him!* My anxiety had subsided. We focused on bringing the white light out of the palms of our hands and imagined it flowing to our friends, surrounding them in it. Gradually, the strong pull we felt to our friends faded. We both collapsed on the bed, exhausted.

"Whew! If this isn't real, if this really didn't happen the way we saw it, I'm giving all of this up," Bob exclaimed. I quickly agreed. We even went as far as saying that if this did happen the way we experienced it, we would never doubt again! We tried to call our friends at home over the next few days but neither of them answered. Finally, they called us. When our woman friend began, "My God, we needed you so badly the other day," Bob told her not to say another word. He related exactly what had happened to them as we had perceived it. It was precisely accurate. She had urgently wanted to call us but couldn't. There was no phone in the room and she didn't want to leave her companion alone.

Our trust in the guides and in our own knowing was greatly strengthened, but lingering doubts remained. Occasionally, when thoughts crept in that I was deluding myself, just imagining my connection with the guides, I would suddenly feel a strong second heartbeat in my chest—a heartbeat in addition to my own! It was so disconcerting to experience two thumping places inside me that I would quickly acknowledge out loud, "Okay, okay! I believe, I believe!"

Little by little I learned to discern when the guides wanted to tell me something even though my mind wasn't focused on them. Normally, my thoughts hummed along in the background, much like a refrigerator motor that isn't heard anymore because of its constancy. The guides' messages, on the other hand, were loud, irregular, and persistent, thoughts that demanded attention. They penetrated my consciousness like the loud thumping of heat going though a radiator.

One morning when I was preparing to leave for work, I "heard" very loudly: *Wear your bright red raincoat.* It was silly, I reasoned. The sky was sunny and clear. But the thought was consistent. Anytime I entertained the idea of wearing my everyday coat, I experienced a pressure bearing down on my head. When I took a moment to focus on the guides and asked them to tell me through automatic writing why I needed to wear the red coat, all I could get was the word "connection." Then the energy in my hand kept switching on and off, moving the pen unevenly. The writing didn't make sense. I couldn't take the time to meditate and try to sort it all out. I left the house with an odd sense of pending doom. I wondered if I'd ever see Bob again. The night before, the word "connection" kept coming to us, but we finally decided it had something to do with the music Bob was writing, a connection in a passage from one part of the piece to another.

On the road I was so busy trying to figure out what this was all about that I almost drove off the highway going around a curve. The suddenness of the near accident brought me back to present time. I fully concentrated on negotiating the heavy traffic going across the Tappen Zee Bridge. It was a relatively narrow bridge for all the cars it had to accommodate, and there were no shoulders to pull off to the side.

Cars were bumper to bumper all the way across, moving at high speed. Suddenly, there was no power to my car! I lost speed rapidly. Instinctively, I thrust my arm out the open window to signal the car behind me. Brakes squealed everywhere. I braced myself, certain that the car behind me would crash into my rear fender. I was so frightened it took me a moment to realize that the bump hadn't happened, and that someone was standing at the window talking to me.

"Boy, it's a good thing you had on that bright red coat or I would never have seen your signal in time to step on the brake," the man said. He was the driver of the car behind me. Fortunately, everyone else behind him had been able to stop safely, also. "Open your hood and let's see what the trouble is," he instructed. He quickly fixed the problem. The connecting wire from the distributor to the engine had come loose, causing the motor to stall immediately. The guides had tried to warn us about the loose connection, but our minds kept trying to put their words into a context we knew. Since they couldn't convey that message clearly to us, the next best thing was to instruct me to wear the red coat.

We learned to let the messages come through fully without trying to anticipate what the guides wanted to say. Our minds became more sensitive, perceiving words before they were written. The guides began communicating through us without automatic writing. We asked a question, then one of us acted as the channel and said the words as they came through. The other wrote down the message. This took great concentration and affected our body temperature. We found ourselves shivering, requiring heavier clothing even when the room temperature was warmer than usual. After a session, we were often famished and needed to eat.

This kind of channeling took less effort when we communicated with what our guides called the "masters." These highly evolved entities, devoted to serving the evolution of humanity and assisting in awakening the consciousness on Earth, came through with a much stronger energy. Our guides introduced us to the master who would work with us. To Zelephius we addressed our deepest questions: What is the purpose of existence? What is God? What is the nature of the soul? The answers were direct and simplified to meet our meager scope of understanding. They blew the bottom out of any theories I had formulated up to that point.

Through the work with the guides and the masters, I realized that no matter how fast the face of the iceberg named Ellen melted to expose another surface, there were always more levels underneath submerged in unconsciousness.

Messages

Bring me my bathrobe, Bob's voice resounded inside my head as I prepared to leave the bathroom and return to the apartment. I snatched Bob's robe off the door hook and stepped across the hallway. "Here's your robe," I said to Bob as I opened the apartment door.

Bob gaped at me incredulously. "It worked!" he said. "I silently sent you the thought to bring me my robe, but I never really expected you to do it!"

Through experimenting with each other, we found we were both adept in sending and receiving messages. When I went to the store to buy milk, I thought I smelled Bob's pipe tobacco. Then quickly got his message: *Buy me some tobacco.* When I went out on some errand and realized I would get home later than I anticipated, I focused on Bob and "spoke" to him with the thought of where I was, that I would be late, not to worry. He would get the message, but still worry!

The idea that we could consciously send thoughts to each other made me wonder if more of my "thinking" than I realized came from my environment, being sent either consciously or unconsciously by other people. In my sessions with Allen, he often talked about how each of us is a part of the environment, and that we influence other people by our thoughts without them ever knowing. Thoughts are energy perceived on the subconscious level, and they affect the nervous system. Clear and positive thoughts create a "clean" environment that makes us feel good. Confused or negative thoughts create a muddled or "polluted" atmosphere that affects our moods, and often how we feel about ourselves.

My natural sense of insecurity and inadequacy was magnified at parties or with large groups of people, where I absorbed everyone else's thoughts and feelings. The barrage on my psyche put me in overload. Not being able to sort out my own thoughts caused me to feel off balance and thus, more insecure. Often I called it "being high on people." It was similar to what I experienced when I had something alcoholic to drink, except that I became hyperactive with nervous energy instead of feeling relaxed and detached. Allen explained that this phenomenon was more pronounced with me than with most people, that I was born with a highly sensitized nervous system that responded to extremely subtle impulses from the environment. Also, my "channel" to the universe was innately open, putting me in an eternal receiving mode. I was a radar receiver continuously picking up anything within range. When this kind of sensitivity is developed gradually through meditation and conscious focus, some control or discrimination of what is to be received evolves simultaneously. I had bypassed this process and, thus, had not learned any conscious control over my receiving.

Not only did I "hear" people's thoughts before they spoke them, but I also told people things about themselves that logically I had no way of knowing. In high school I was called Mother Ellen because I counseled my peers about their relationships with their parents or boy friends whom I had never met. More than once I was asked, "How do you know all of that?" At the time I chalked it off to having aborbed the maturity and wisdom of my three older sisters. But when I thought about it later, this explanation didn't make much sense. Only one of my sisters was around while I was growing up. In college I was questioned by my professors when I talked or wrote about things that they didn't think I had any way of knowing. My child psychology professor took me aside to talk about a paper I wrote. I was to recommend a play program for a child in the preschool after observing him for two weeks. As a reason for my recommedations, I had written a summary of the child's relationship to his parents, whom I had never met. "They happen to be my very good friends and you are totally accurate!" she exclaimed. From then on she asked me about the other children and what I thought their relationships to their parents were. She was thoroughly impressed and gave me an "A" for the course.

I never understood the fuss other people made about my knowing. I thought all these things were very obvious. In college, a graduate student, whom I had a crush on, was writing his history master's thesis. When he confided one evening over dinner that he was frustrated with his writing and didn't know how to continue his paper, I asked him to tell me a bit about it. He sat there with his mouth wide open as I proceeded to instruct him about what the next chapters needed to be. He couldn't believe an underclassman could be so smart! But for me it was easy, a natural progression. At the time I didn't think twice about it, but in retrospect it seems that occasionally all I needed to do was to focus my mind on a specific subject and information came automatically, without any logical source. When my friends discussed politics, in which I had no interest nor ever read about in the newspapers, I could easily and accurately describe the personal qualities of the politicians and comment on what I liked about them and what I didn't. At the time I never questioned why I knew these things; rather, I questioned why other people didn't.

When Bob and I compared our perceptions about other people, we found they were very different. Bob talked about appearance, manner of speaking, sense of humor, temperament and skill. I talked about intentions, desires, fears, and happiness. How could our assessments be so different? It was more than just being different people with different priorities. I became acutely aware that my perceptions weren't "normal." Bob's observations were about outer expression, what most people observed. Mine were of the more subtle, inner being that I automatically perceived through my sensitivity. In fact, the more obvious attributes that Bob observed often escaped my notice all together. My radar gave me strong impressions about the inner nature that apparently pre-empted my comprehension of more tangible (to other people) qualities. This was especially obvious when a new acquaintance visited us. After he left, I told Bob what a nice person the man was and expounded on why this was so. Bob was flabbergasted. "Ellen, the guy's a bastard!" He pointed out all the obvious reasons he based his opinion on. Once I thought about it, I could see that if judged merely by his behavior and his words, I would have to agree with Bob, the man was arrogant and obnoxious. But I had missed that. I was more attuned to the caring, gentleness and integrity that he wasn't expressing.

It dawned on me, perhaps for the first time, that other people—as well as myself—had a discrepancy between their "true" selves and their personality, that most people have an inner reality that is not conveyed to the world by their outer expression. This discrepancy certainly explained why I was so often disappointed with people. I automatically discerned a person's potential and expected to have the person live it fully. Most often, actions and behaviors fell far short of the possibilities I felt and hoped for. I was attuned to the higher-selves of people far more than I was to their personalities, or outer-selves. It was I who was missing the "obvious!"

This realization was a blow to my ego. How could I be so unaware? I began focusing more on the "obvious." Bob was a big help in pointing it out. He had a mind for details and gloried in logically coming to conclusions about what he observed. Lessons were to go both ways, however. The more Bob developed his sensitivities with meditation and work with the guides, the more he experienced the higher qualities of people. The realistic view was a combination of the two realities: to acknowledge the urges of the higher self, while being aware that pure expression is modified by the fears and limitations we live in. Of course, observing this in other people helped both of us to see it more clearly in ourselves.

We watched for emotional or behavioral patterns that hindered our true expression. Bob realized his impatience impeded his growth. His tendency to rush everywhere and do everything in a hurry obstructed opportunities for expressing his creativity and for perceiving the nuances of life. It also caused friction in his relationships, with his cohorts as well as with me. I hated to be hustled out of the house every time we went anywhere. Inevitably, Bob, in his haste, forgot something and had to dash back into the house while I waited angrily in the car. His impatience with other drivers on the road resulted in some close calls and certainly jangled my nerves. The guides insisted he train himself to be patient both with others and himself. He took their advice to heart and disciplined himself. He prayed for traffic jams just so he could practice patience!

For myself, I realized behaviors centered around my feelings of inadequacy hindered my full expression. In my temporary secretarial jobs, I found myself explaining my "true" identity to each new staff I worked with. I wanted people to know I wasn't "just" a secretary. I had held important, creative jobs in the past. I told about writing for *Farm Journal* and being on TV in Boston. Of course my fellow workers were impressed, but I also found they resented me, with good reason. By pumping myself up, I was implying they were inferior to me. When I recognized this, I was embarrassed and explored the reasons for my behavior. I realized I felt ashamed about not using my full potential all the time. I had skills that I could be using for much higher paying jobs than secretarial ones and felt guilty about working below my capacity. Bob inadvertently contributed to this by always describing me as "a writer" to our friends. Although I enjoyed writing, I was trained as a journalist and I never thought of myself as a writer. Being labeled "writer" made me feel I *should* be writing. The fact that I wasn't and didn't have the desire to at the time made me feel inadequate, somehow. By letting everyone know that I didn't have to work as a secretary, that I had a choice, was my way of justifying the discrepancy to myself.

It was my choice to have more time with Bob rather than the higher pay of a more demanding job.

Being together was my top priority. Telling fellow workers about glamor jobs I'd held boosted my ego when I felt insecure, reassuring myself of my capabilities, but I certainly didn't feel superior to anyone else and felt badly to have created that impression. It wasn't at all what I wanted to express.

Once I realized what I was doing, I chose to stop it. I made a pact with myself that I would no longer volunteer information about my past to my fellow workers. Instead, I would open more to who they were and show interest in their lives, get them to talk about themselves rather than talk about myself. Since I changed jobs often, I had lots of practice, and the results were good. The other workers accepted me more readily and more often asked about my life. I could share much more than I could before, and was more of who I was at the moment rather than who I was in the past.

Subtle Realities

Bob was embarrassed when I told other people about our work with the guides, especially when I was so casual about it. He felt it wasn't the kind of information most people could receive easily, and that I should be more discriminating about whom I told. Perhaps he was right, but I found that most people who knew me well, or who had at least experienced my down-to-earth, practical manner, were receptive to the idea of guides, if I mentioned them matter-of-factly rather than made it a big mystery. I trusted that if I found myself talking to someone about guides, I knew they were ready for the information.

The first thing people wanted to know was whether they themselves had guides. When we affirmed that everyone had at least an inner guide, the next question was, "Who is my guide?" Bob and I received the answer to this through automatic writing. "Does my guide have anything to tell me?" took more concentration to answer. One of us went into another room and let the inquirer's guide write through us. The message was often several pages long. To have these messages gratefully received and their appropriateness acknowledged was another confirmation of the guide's validity. We were still somewhat skeptical that information that came this easily could be accurate. We also worried about our objectivity, especially for people we knew well. To test ourselves, we each asked for a message for the same person and then compared our results. The information always coincided. Another way to assure accuracy was to check with our own guides. Bob would ask me to check any messages he got with Allen and I would ask Bob to check my messages with his guide. This became standard procedure for all our guide communications.

Gradually word got around that Bob and I "did readings." Friends of friends started to call us. We asked for a message from the guides and the person requesting a reading would come to pick it up. It was always a strange experience for me to have such intimate information for someone I never met. While receiving the information through automatic writing I tried to attune myself to the person the reading was for. I often sensed their present state of mind, their emotions, their torments, and their desires. Then, when I first met the person, it always took a moment or two to match my preconceived picture with the reality standing in front of me; to adjust the inner reality I experienced with the outer appearance.

I had a real scare one time when I arranged to drop off a reading at a man's antique store. I introduced myself and while we talked I began to have major doubts about the validity of the reading. I couldn't imagine that this radiant, happy man could have the distressing concerns and deep suffering indicated in the reading. I felt a complete fool and dreaded handing the reading to him. Thank goodness he has busy with a customer and asked if I could come back in fifteen minutes. Panicked, I ran to the nearest telephone and called Bob. I asked him to recheck the accuracy of the reading with his guide. In a few minutes, Bob replied that the reading was right and would be very helpful. For the few minutes remaining before I needed to return to the antique store, I paced the aisles of a supermarket, trying to quell my anxiety. When at last it was time to make the presentation of the reading, I took a deep breath and handed it to the man. He asked me to have a seat while he went into another room to read the message from his guide. In a few minutes he returned with tears streaming down his face. He gave me a big hug and thanked me from the bottom of his heart. He was suffering major conflict in his life and the information in the reading was what he needed to help him through it. I quietly thanked the guides for coming through so brilliantly and asked them, once again, to forgive me for my doubts.

Giving readings was time consuming. It took an hour or more to receive the information, and then another hour at least to meet with the person and go over the reading. To be more efficient I tried a different approach. Instead of receiving so much information through automatic writing from the guides ahead of time, I tried meditating and attuning myself to the person just before they arrived, and then, with the person present, I said what I perceived and opened to any additional information the guides wished to impart. Their information came through me via thoughts, pictures, feelings, and, occasionally, voices. This method improved the more I relied on it, and eventually I dispensed with automatic writing entirely, receiving all information directly in the person's presence.

Both Bob and I continued to feel insecure enough that we still depended on the reassurance of each other's checking for the accuracy of each reading. We often used our fingers instead of a pen when we asked the guides to give us a "yes" or "no" by automatic writing, using an arm, a leg, or a table top for our paper. Sometimes in my commute to work I used this method to check the messages I received as I drove. I silently asked Allen for verification by giving him control of my finger to write a yes or no answer on the steering wheel. Sometimes, if I questioned whether it was truly Allen writing through my finger, the scent of gardenias would suddenly fill the car as a way of confirmation. What a strange phenomenon to smell gardenias when surrounded by the exhaust fumes of a New York rush hour!

We found that all our normal outer senses, hearing, sight, touch, taste, and smell, had comparable inner senses that could be developed and used consciously. We could *hear* the voices of the guides in our heads, we could *see* images that imparted information to us during meditation, we could *feel* presences and energy or whether something was right or wrong, and we could *smell* Allen's gardenias or other scents that helped relay information to us. The way we developed these sensitivities was through meditation and use; relying on these senses readily to communicate with the inner reality.

Meditation helped to focus our attention on our inner space and the subtler levels of consciousness; we remained conscious of the physical world but disengaged from it. Even when there were loud noises, or we had a headache, the more we focused on our inner selves, the less noticeable these outer things were. Frequently we came back to "normal" consciousness after meditating for awhile and were surprised at how cold and dark the room was and how loud the traffic outside sounded.

I once had the experience of waiting in a busy train station with friends who had come to see me off and were gaily talking among themselves. When I was concerned about hearing the loudspeaker announce my train, I didn't hear what my friends were saying. When I concentrated specifically on their conversation, however, I heard the loudspeaker only as background noise; I didn't comprehend the words. It was a matter of focus, as was meditating or attuning to the guides. When I concentrated on my inner hearing, I perceived the guides' messages even when the room was filled with other sounds. When I focused on my inner sight, I saw pictures in my head without closing my eyes.

As I developed my sensitivities, I perceived subtler realities. When I noticed a ring of colors around sheets of music, the guides told me these were etheric energy bodies, or auras, which indicated the qualities of life force inherent in the music. Even when music isn't actually played, the written notes have a subtle influence on the environment by the energy put into it by the composer. I drew the colors I saw around music to create an aura picture, and then attuned to the colors to feel their differing moods or emotions. I could then compare the music of various composers or the different pieces of the same composer. I found that each composer had a trademark aura that differed only slightly from piece to piece. I also began seeing auras around people. It was with my inner eye rather than my physical eye that I usually saw them, so that the picture would be in my head, not in front of me. Sometimes, however, I saw them with my physical eyes, too, so that the aura appeared as an extended part of the person's physical body.

Perceiving auras or the energy fields around people aided us in our healing work. We not only sent light, or energy, as we did for Dr. Fritz, but we also learned to pass energy through the different levels of the aura. This helped renew physical energy or helped clear out anything that was held in the subtler levels of consciousness that contributed to the ailment or illness of the person we were working on. Often there were negative thoughts, emotions, or beliefs that needed to be acknowledged and then released. These we perceived with our inner senses as we passed our hands through the aura.

We often doubted the impressions we received and cautiously shared them with the person we were working on. We were amazed that these were readily accepted as being accurate and that the person's condition usually improved immediately.

It was a startling discovery for me to find that what I thought or believed affected my physical well-being. I realized that my belief that it was inevitable to get a cold each winter was reinforced by the media advertisements for cold and flu remedies—"When you get your cold (or flu) this winter, reach for. . ." Without fail, I got my expected bad cold or flu each year. Our healing work helped me see how I set myself up. I unconsciously retained a belief that my body responded to. By changing my belief, I could change what affected my body. Becoming aware of my belief and realizing I didn't have to get sick was the first step. Choosing to be well was the second.

After this revelation, the first time I began to feel a cold coming on, a sore throat and whoosy feeling, I decided to do something about it before it became a full-blown cold. I really didn't want to be sick. I meditated and then imagined white light flowing into my aura as I passed my hands over my body, just as I would if I were working on someone else. Immediately, I felt the warmth of the light in my head, throat, and chest. I imagined the light burning the soreness out and health being restored. I continued until I felt a releasing sensation and knew the healing was complete.

It occurred to me, then, that my body had responded to something, a belief, emotion, or thought, to allow me to get a sore throat. Since I no longer believed I had to get sick, there had to be some other cause. When I asked myself what I could gain by being sick, the answer was "rest." I was exhausted but didn't know how to say "no" to the continual demands on my time and energy. During the week, I worked all day, came home, made dinner, and then went with Bob to band rehearsals or performances. On weekends I did housework, the shopping, paid the bills and spent time with Bob. I had no time for myself. Being sick gave me a good excuse to do what I really wanted to do; to blob out, not do anything. Once I discovered my body was responding to my unconscious desire for rest, I choose a happier solution. Instead, of having to get sick to stay in bed, I gave myself permission to take a rest anytime I wanted, even when there was work to do (there was *always* work to do!). Then, by making good health a top priority, I gave myself the authority to say no to activities I knew were taxing my energy. It was the first winter I could remember that I didn't get a cold.

California

When we heard that Dr. Halloway, a well-regarded psychic, was to give a talk locally, we jumped at the opportunity to hear him. Although he spoke with a religious bent, we found much that he talked about confirmed many of the ideas that our guides had revealed or we had discovered for ourselves. The portion of his presentation that especially intrigued us was his clairvoyant perceptions of the people in the audience. We laughed when he "read" Bob accurately, calling him a "bold spirit," but when he predicted Bob would move to California the following May, we sat open mouthed. Even more so when the woman sitting next to Bob warned, "If Dr. Halloway says you are going to move, you'd better pack your bags!"

We had no intention, or desire to move to California, so we weren't surprised that May came and went and we were still in Nyack. We liked Nyack but were living there mainly because of its close proximity to New York. Bob could work with his band in the city while we enjoyed a relaxed life in Nyack. Our real dream was to live in New Hampshire in a big, old New England farmhouse. Even though Bob's band played at some of the New York clubs, we were beginning to realize the pay wasn't worth sticking around for, especially when a recording contract wasn't forthcoming. Also, Bob's hopes for having his compositions played by one of the contempory groups in New York hadn't materialized.

We planned weekend trips to New Hampshire to visit friends and look for jobs. We agreed it was important for Bob to have time to compose, and he needed a job that would allow that. A physically active job might combine well with composing, perhaps working on a farm. We explored the possibilities without results. I wanted some kind of editing work and applied to *Yankee Magazine* and to *New Hampshire Profiles*, but, again, to no avail. Meanwhile, I continued in the job I had taken as a reports clerk for AT&T in Mt. Kisco until something else presented itself.

Our hope of going to New Hampshire had faded by the time a percussionist friend, Maruga, called Bob. He was in California playing music with friends, and wondered if Bob would come and complete their quartet. Bob decided to go and feel the situation out.

It was the first time since we were married that Bob and I were separated. We called each other every day. Thank goodness AT&T paid a percentage of our long distance calls as a job benefit or our bill would have been exorbitant! At first we called only because we missed each other, but as time passed we found that the main focus of our calls was to check each other's readings. Suddenly, we were both in high demand. Bob gave readings to Maruga and the other musicians, their spouses and friends, and I had become popular at AT&T.

As Bob focused more on activities in California, and I socialized more frequently with people I met at work, we found we were too busy to check our individual readings with each other. We could no longer call daily to check each reading as we gave it. Instead, we coordinated our calls as best we could to give blanket checks on all the readings we had given since the last time we talked. Finally, we realized that perhaps we had been too dependent on each other, that from then on we would only verify the most crucial information.

Bob's excitement with the group in California grew until he finally decided it would be worth our while to move to Los Angeles. As soon as he returned to Nyack we began making our plans. We sold or gave away all of our belongings except what fit into our Volvo, and by the beginning of May (a year later than Dr. Halloway's prediction) we were on our way to California.

At first we stayed with the pianist and his wife, Darius and Sheena Brubeck, in their Hollywood Hills apartment, but as soon as we could, we looked for a place of our own. Having no income for the time being, we decided we didn't want to pay more than $125 a month in rent. We also agreed we wanted a house rather than an apartment. Everyone thought we were crazy, thinking we could find such an inexpensive house in Hollywood, but Bob and I, relying on our many previous experiences, declared boldly that anything is possible. All we needed to do was to decide what we wanted and go for it.

Our optimism faded, however, when our intense search turned up nothing. It was hard enough to find a house at all to rent in Hollywood, much less one for $125 a month. Reluctantly, we checked out apartments and found a small studio for $150 a month that would suffice if we couldn't find anything else. We told the landlord we would give him a final answer later that day, and drove down the street feeling disappointed. The studio apartment wasn't right, but what else could we do? We wanted a place immediately.

Then we both spotted a small "for rent" sign stuck into the lawn of a tiny cottage. We knew instinctively this was it! We stopped and ran up to the door. The house for rent, we were informed, was behind this one and the rent was $125. Bob and I gave each other an aha! look and tried to suppress our excitement. This *was* it! Our hopes fell, however, with our first glimpse inside the house—it was dark, dirty and smelled of insecticide—but as we inspected the rooms we began to visualize how nicely it could be fixed up. There was plenty of space, a large front room, a bedroom and a good sized kitchen. There were no appliances, however. We would have to buy these. The yard was small but pleasant with a large avocado tree and several hibiscus bushes. The house was between two other similar houses, away from the street and noisy traffic, and safe for our dog. We paid our first month's rent and were given the keys. There was no lease and no security deposit. The place was ours! The neighbors told us that the house had been used to make pornographic films and that they had sometimes acted in them. Great! This was Hollywood!

We immediately set to work making our little house into a home. First we washed every available surface, then painted. We found a used refrigerator and an antique gas stove, the kind with legs. I made over some old curtains we brought with us, and we bought a new mattress. We looked in used furniture stores for a couch and chairs but didn't see anything that we liked or that we could afford. On the way to visit Sheena and Darius one day, I discovered a desk that had been put on the curb to be picked up by the garbage truck. Then I found a couch and table and some decorative pillows. I couldn't believe what treasures people threw out. Before long I picked up some chairs and a lamp—all for free! From then on I kept a list of everything we wanted and waited for the weekly trash days when everyone put their garbage out on the curb. Then, while Bob rehearsed, I scrounged the streets, picking up all the items on my list. To Bob's amazement, I always found exactly what we needed.

One week we had a particularly long and specific list, including molding strips to finish off a closet and screens for the non-standard, irregular windows in the front room. I roamed the hilly streets of Hollywood, picking up my loot, ignoring the stares I received as I stopped the car in front of promising piles and nonchalantly rummaged through them. I pretended I was in a department store looking at all the merchandise, comparing items and selecting only the best. At the end of the day, I proudly anticipated Bob's reaction to my success of finding almost everything on the list, even the molding strips for the closet. I hadn't, however, found the screens. I wondered for a moment where else I might look and found myself turning down a street I had never been on before. There, a man with a bewildered look on his face carried a long narrow window screen to the curb. I quickly pulled over and rolled my window down. "Are you throwing that screen out?" I asked. Indeed he was. Then I asked if he had, by chance, a second screen. Yes, he did, and yes, I could have them both.

As the man helped me load the screens in my already full car, he said, "It's the oddest thing. I've had these screens in my garage for years and suddenly, just a few minutes ago, I had this urge to throw them out!"

I could hardly wait to see Bob's face when he saw my loot! I also wanted to hurry home to see if the screens fit the windows as I was so sure they would. Bob was pleased to see the results of my "shopping" as he helped me unload the car. He was truly amazed when the screens fit perfectly. But then he said that I had forgotten something. I couldn't imagine what. The rug for the living room, Bob informed me. Sure enough, I had missed it on the list. "Well, let's go get it!" I said. We both hopped into the car and drove to the top of a hill. There, curbside, was a large beige rug in good condition except for some minor fading. Within 15 minutes we were back home trying out our new living room rug!

As our house filled up with my trash pickings, I quit looking for specific items and hunted for treasures instead, looking for anything unusual. It was odd how when I wasn't looking for anything in particular, the pickings were slim, just garbage. After several weeks of not finding much, Bob said he wanted me to look for a chair for him. He had a particular kind of chair in mind, but he wouldn't tell me what it was. He told me to find a chair I thought he would like. The next trash day I went out and saw nothing but chairs! There was every kind of chair you could imagine, from classic upholstered to modern sculpted plastic. Only one chair caught my eye, however. It had a light wood frame with stretched hide on the seat and curved back. I loaded it in the car and headed home. It was the only chair I picked up. Bob's mouth fell open as he stared at the chair. It was the exact one he wanted!

The next week I decided I wanted a chair, too. The fancy wicker kind with a tall circular back. Bob wanted a round picnic table for the yard. I easily found both items, but then Bob realized he had forgotten to tell me to find an umbrella to go with the table. I found that the next week. Bob began to brag about my ability to manifest our needs in the trash. Soon I had a list of things to find for our frugal friends. Never before had I seen children's clothes, but the next week I filled Sheena's request for dresses for her daughter. I found several the right size in good condition.

The universe, it seemed, was a good provider. All we needed to do was decide what we wanted. One of our most frequent requests was money. Whenever our coffers were especially low, we both worried. Then, without letting the other know, we each put in a call to the universe. We were afraid that talking about our requests would somehow decrease the possibility of having it manifest. Too, neither Bob nor I wanted the other to know we were worrying! Invariably our money requests brought almost instant results—all the quicker when both of us requested at the same time. Money came from all different sources: a long forgotten utility deposit check or payment on a loan from a friend, an unexpected check from one of our parents, or a door prize from some special event. We never knew how our request would be filled and didn't specify. We believed the universe was filled with options that our limited minds could never imagine and that to be too specific about how our desires were fulfilled would limit the possibilities. Always, the money would tide us over until our next earned money came.

One thing we soon learned was that the timing of the universe was different from our timing. Usually, when we wanted something, it was now! The universe had other ideas, ones we didn't always understand at the time. Not long after we moved to California, Bob's request to have his music played was answered. He received a letter from an organization of musicians in New York that played unknown composers' works. They wanted to play one of Bob's pieces and would pay him $200. The only stipulation was that he would have to be present for the performance. Since it wasn't practical for Bob to fly to New York at the time, he couldn't take advantage of the opportunity. Poor Bob, how he lamented. I tried to comfort him with words of wisdom, how the universe knows best and how sometimes when one door closes another even better one opens.

The next week, it was my turn. I received a letter from *New Hampshire Profiles* magazine offering me a job as associate editor. My dream job! Poor Ellen, how she lamented. Bob offered me comfort (not words of wisdom!). He hugged me and said he knew how I felt.

Once we were established in our little house, I registered with the same temporary job agency I worked for in New York and immediately began working for various companies in Los Angeles. Bob spent his days rehearsing with the band. The band became our nuclear family. We ate together, played together, and counseled each other. We also meditated together. Maruga, Darius and Sheena, and Ken, the bass player, were all as spiritually oriented as ourselves. Maruga was a follower of Swami Satchidananda; Darius and Sheena were involved in Scientology; and Ken, who sampled many paths, practiced Tai Chi and Fruitarianism (he only ate fruit). Since our combined experience was diverse, we had much to share with each other. Maruga took us to his ashram, Darius and Sheena ran some of the Scientology processes on us, and Ken taught us Tai Chi. Bob and I led meditations and helped the others get in touch with their guides. Perhaps because of the intensity of our group, unusual experiences were common.

Several times when Maruga and I were together, a flash of bright yellow light passed between us, followed by a wonderful feeling of compassion for each other. We had the sense of knowing each other before and decided we had been brother and sister in another lifetime. The experience climaxed when we were visiting Maruga's ashram. We were with a group eating dinner on a cloth spread out on the floor. Maruga and I sat together and happened to glance at each other as I lifted a forkful of food to my mouth. Suddenly, a knowing of a former lifetime came to us simultaneously. At the exact same instant we each dropped our forks and yelled, "Gypsies!" Falling into each other's arms, we blurted out details of our life together as gypsies while the people around us gaped with amazement. We had the exact same memory. A reporter who was eating with us was so intimidated by the experience, he bolted from the room.

Another incident began one night when a group of us was preparing to meditate. Ken entered the house in a daze. He had just passed a woman on the street whom he had dreamt about on several occasions previously but whom he didn't know and had never seen before. She stopped and watched him staring at her and asked him, "Where are you going?"

He replied, "In there," pointing to our house.

No sooner had he finished telling us the story when there was a knock at the door. It was the woman Ken had dreamt about. She asked if she could come in. After seeing Ken on the street, she sensed she needed to go where he was going. She asked what we were doing and we explained that we were about to meditate. She suggested that we might be able to help her. She had been having many frightening occurrences in her house. Her lights went on by themselves after she turned them off, she found boxes from the closet shelf dumped out on her bed, she heard heavy breathing by her ear at night, and her rocking chair rocked by itself as if someone was in it. There were no logical explanations. Was she going mad?

When the group focused on her problem, Bob and I looked at each other. We both received the same answer. . . a ghost! Neither he nor I believed in ghosts but our guides had confirmed that ghosts do exist. That sometimes a soul gets trapped in an astral existence after an unsettling life on earth or a tragic death, or sometimes a person who dies is especially attached to earth life and doesn't want to move on. This was our first experience with this kind of situation. The ghost we perceived was that of an actor who had died in the woman's apartment. He was drunk and somehow knocked a tall, heavy bookcase over on top of himself and died. The actor's name was George. We advised the woman to tell George he could have one of the rooms in the apartment for himself if he promised not to bother her. He apparently didn't like the fact that she was there and was trying to frighten her into leaving. We encouraged her not to give into her fear. Instead of being intimidated by his scare tactics, she should try to talk George into moving on.

The woman stayed in touch with us. She checked with the landlord and the neighbors as to whether there had ever been an actor in that apartment. As far as anyone could remember there had been an actor living there years before, he was a heavy drinker, and apparently, had died there, but no one was clear as to the circumstances. The woman then talked to George and offered him the smallest room in the apartment, agreeing she wouldn't go in there, but only on the condition he would behave. The lights hadn't gone on since, the boxes remained in the closet, and the heavy breathing at night had stopped—but the rocking chair still rocked!

Not long after the meditation night, I was sitting at my receptionist desk in a one-girl office. I felt a presence around me and asked silently who was there. I took out a pen and paper expecting to get a message from one of our guides. Instead, it was George! He was angry at me for exposing him to the woman. She was no longer afraid of him, he complained. I told him he was not doing himself any good by hanging around the earth plane, it was time to move on. Bob and I and the meditation group sent him light hoping it would help him let go of his earth attachment. Not long after, even the rocking chair quit rocking.

The meditation group had two other very dramatic experiences. The first occurred at one of our first meetings. There were about 10 of us meditating, using the form of meditation that the guides recommended. We visualized a column of white light going to a group of master souls who redirected the light back to the earth plane where it was used for the best good of humanity. Sometimes we were told or shown, and on this particular night, "taken" to where the light was being used. We found ourselves witnessing a secret meeting with President Nixon and the Chinese government. We were instructed (by the masters) to visualize various situations to aid the meeting. None of us could quite believe our perceptions, and yet it all felt very real. At the end of the meditation, we were told that the secret meeting would be revealed in the newspapers within ten days. Indeed, within that time the historic meeting was the main story in all the media!

During another group meditation, we had the startling experience of having Zeliphius, our master guide, materialize before our eyes. It was our dog who alerted us to something unusual going on. He suddenly stood up from where he was lying and darted into the center of our circle. He began growling as the figure of a robed, white-haired man began to appear. We knew instantly that this tall stately man bathed in light was Zeliphius. Our dog continued to growl until Zeliphius bent over and began petting him! Then he wagged his tail and sat calmly at Zeliphius's feet. Zeliphius greeted us briefly (through our inner ears) and then disappeared.

Bob and I wondered whether the frequency of unusual, often psychic experiences we had in California had to do with the lighter vibration we felt there. The north eastern part of the country, New England and New York, seemed much heavier. Perhaps the greater population with a much longer history accounted for what we experienced as a heavy accumulation of mental activity. California, on the the other hand, felt young, more physically oriented and spontaneous. It seemed easier to be creative and imaginative there, with things quicker to take hold. People seemed more open minded, less judgmental. The Northeast on the other hand, felt more secure and, although projects were harder to get started, once they were going were more apt to endure. In California ideas were abundant, but the actions they inspired didn't last long. I felt very happy, creative and carefree in California.

It seemed, too, that everyone we met in California was on some kind of spiritual path. We heard many different claims to having THE WAY to spiritual enlightenment and were amused by the many people who tried to convert us to their path. Diet was a big issue. Bob and I were real meat and potato eaters, a no-no among the people we met. You had to be vegetarian, or macrobiotic, or some other exotic variation in order to be "spiritual." We enjoyed the many different meals our friends prepared for us in hopes of persuading us to their diet inclination. One friend, in particular, nagged us continually about eating differently. Finally, to get him off our backs, I told him I had been guided to the perfect diet. I needed to eat only things that were white—egg whites, white flour, white sugar, salt, yogurt and cottage cheese. Triumphant at last, he took me seriously for a few days and praised me profusely for changing my heathen ways!

Being around so many creative people brought out my feelings of inadequacy. Bob and the other musicians had their music and Sheena wrote poetry. I worked most days and had little time for creative endeavors. I asked the guides for help in developing something I could share artistically. As I waited for a reply through automatic writing, my pen began making a continuous flowing line. Up and down, around and around, changing direction abruptly, duplicating movements contiguously, until finally returning to the original starting point. The result was an intricate design that filled the paper without one single break. Automatic drawing! Excitedly, I put the pen down on another piece of paper. Again, the same continuous line formed a complicated design without ever crossing itself or breaking. Bob called my new art form "psychotic art. " Indeed, the drawings were intense and somehow mesmerizing. I softened the effect and added dimension with colored pencil and watercolor. The enhanced designs brought enthusiastic praises from my friends.

At an office where I worked as a temporary for several months, I discussed reincarnation and my experiences with the guides with one of the executives. He was understandably skeptical about communication with invisible entities. When he confided that he was an aspiring artist, I asked him to witness my automatic drawing. While he watched, I held a pen at the very tip with my thumb and forefinger affording me minimal control. I relaxed my arm and let the pen glide across the paper forming a flowing design. My friend was totally transfixed. "God," he exclaimed, "I wish I had that kind of control with a paintbrush!"

After many months of rehearsing, the band was ready to perform. They called themselves the Darius Brubeck Quartet, capitalizing on the fame of Darius's father, Dave Brubeck, the jazz pianist. Their debut in a Los Angeles club evoked an enthusiastic response from the audience but a negative review by the Los Angeles music critic, Leonard Feather. When Dave heard this he was delighted and told the group, "If

Leonard Feather doesn't like you, you must be hot!" Indeed, shortly after their California debut, the group was booked for a trial run at Trudy Heller's, the well-known New York club.

With less than a week to get to New York, Bob and I packed our essentials and, except for one long nap at a motel along the way, drove non-stop to New York. Arriving in the wake of a hurricane and with the car limping along on burned-out valves, we persisted on to Boston. We wanted to see Mom and Dad Fritz and pick up their Volkswagen camper that would be our home base in New York.

Opening week at Trudy Heller's was exciting, especially so because the Darius Brubeck Quartet was well received. Sitting proudly at my table, I spent the week surveying the audience and keeping my ears perked for indications of approval or disapproval of the band. At breaks I went out with the group to get something to eat and to discuss their performance. At the end of their trial period, the band was asked to stay on.

Tiring of cigarette smoke and of men trying to pick me up, I spent less time in the club each night and more time in the camper. There I read, slept or worked on my automatic drawings until the guys came to get me at breaks.

The increased focus on my artwork kept me centered amid the schizophrenic energy of New York. The more I worked on my drawings, the easier they flowed. Several people who had taken the finished drawings home told me the designs and colors made them feel good, that they seemed to have a healing effect. When I started to get requests to draw something for specific people, I opened to "whatever was needed" and allowed the design to come through. Sometimes an especially strong urge compelled me to draw even without a specific request. When this happened, I remained in a trance-like mood until the drawing was completed. I knew whoever needed the healing affects of the drawing would come into my life soon.

When the stint at Trudy Heller's ended, the group relocated to Darius's father's house in Wilton, Connecticut. There we were comfortably housed in Dave's large Japanese-styled home. As the group rehearsed, I took advantage of the beautiful woodland setting, dabbling my feet in the pond while I drew. This was an especially enjoyable and creative time for me as I relished the excitement of the music integrated with the spiritual growth of our "family. " My role as mom kept me busy providing encouraging words and counseling, as well as meals. With as many of us as there were, combined with the artistic temperament of the group, there was never a dull moment. The promise of success for the quartet made everything even more pleasurable, of course, and was further enhanced by Dave's enthusiasm. After another well-received performance, this time in Washington, D.C., Dave began helping with the bookings.

One of the first he arranged was at the Holiday Inn in New Haven.

When we heard this news, Bob and I looked at each other and laughed! This was the same hotel that Jack bought right before Bob and I were married. Each time we passed it when we drove between New York and Boston, Bob turned down my suggestion to stop and let me introduce him to Jack. Although Jack had called several times when we lived in Nyack and talked to Bob, they never met. When I encouraged Jack to visit both of us, and he still insisted on seeing me alone, I asked him not to call anymore. The feelings between us were still there, and even though I no longer had the desire to be with him, my dreams indicated I hadn't totally let go of him, either. I dreamed frequently about having to choose between Bob and Jack. I always chose Bob, but not without deliberation. As time passed, the dreams occurred less often and the emotional conflict diminished. The unexpected prospect of seeing Jack at the Holiday Inn stirred old feelings and fears. How would we be with each other after several years of absence?

On the way to the Holiday Inn the night the band was playing, I realized I no longer felt anxious about seeing Jack. I told Bob I didn't think he would be there. As soon as we arrived, I left Bob to set up with the band and went to the hotel lobby. When I spotted an official-looking person, I asked him who the innkeeper was. "I am, " he replied. Somewhat relieved and at the same time disappointed, I asked about Jack and found he had sold the hotel the year before.

When the band began to fly around the country, I stayed with Mom and Dad Fritz in Winthrop and helped with the group's publicity. After high hopes, the quartet went through several changes of personnel and eventually merged with Dave's group. Although Bob cherished the opportunity to play with this jazz giant, he yearned to play his own music. He left Dave and started making himself known in the Boston area. Our lives were filled with rehearsals, jams and concerts for Bob Fritz and Friends, and also for the contemporary quartet that began playing Bob's compositions. It was exciting and rewarding to have Bob's talents recognized at last. I participated as much as I could, toting equipment, monitoring sound balance, and critiquing performances. My main role, however, was that of cheerleader.

The Meditation Group

The transient state of our first years of marriage began to wear on us. Yearning to settle into a home of our own, but not being able to afford more than an apartment, we were grateful when allowed to move into Bob's grandparents' old, two-story Victorian house in Chelsea, an older area of Boston. The home had been empty in the six months since Bob's grand-mother had been placed in a nursing home, and needed a good cleaning. It was filled with at least sixty years of accumulation, all of which we crowded into one of the three bedrooms and into the basement to be dealt with later. The whole house needed to be re-vitalized. To accelerate the process we invited several of our friends to a marathon painting party and were soon basking in our "new" home. With relief we settled in, knowing we could live there as long as we wanted to. The stability renewed our sense of well-being and helped generate the energy we needed for our expanding spiritual work.

As our reputation for our readings grew, a steady stream of spiritual seekers from all around the Boston area knocked at our door. Our popularity was fueled by the meditation group Bob's former composition professor and his charismatic pianist friend asked us to lead. Most of the 10 to 20 people who attended were their students. The group focused on being of service to the world and met weekly. Each newcomer was introduced flamboyantly by the pianist. Once she had proclaimed their special talents and summarized her perception of their spiritual state of affairs, she handed their soul over to me. I was expected to give them a short reading before the meditation began.

When everyone was seated in a big circle, Bob spoke briefly on some subject he received inspiration for during the week or in the car on the way over. Then the lights were lowered and I took incense around to sensitize the inner senses and help bring unity to the group. Bob usually lead the first part of the meditation in which we directed energy to the master souls, the Masters of the White Brotherhood, for their use in aiding humanity's evolution.

As we focused the light to the masters, we often received helpful information for the group as a whole or for specific individuals. Bob and I encouraged participants to express what they experienced instead of holding back; overcoming their self-consciousness and saying the thoughts, feelings, and images that came spontaneously. This participation helped strengthen the individual's connection to the inner self and enriched the group experience by making it more meaningful. It was often that someone hesitant to speak found that once they overcame their shyness, images and information came easier and more frequently. By talking about their perceptions, they released them and could be more receptive to the flow of additional insights. The trick was not to be attached to having the information be right or to judge it.

The information that came to the group was usually about how the light we were channeling was being used, about situations in the world that needed help. Sometimes, though, the guides redirected the energy back to the group to help our spiritual growth, both at the group and individual levels.

Although overall service to the world was the main purpose of the meditation, healing and personal growth were the two secondary focuses. After the first guided part of the meditation, we directed healing energy toward individuals who requested it but were not present. First, we envisioned the person as if they were in the room. Then the group directed the light to one specified member who funneled it to the higher self of the person requesting it. This created a potent pool of extra energy for the person to draw on in whatever ways would be most beneficial. Often, too, we received information about the person's physical symptoms and emotional or psychological condition along with advice which could help remedy their situation. Or, sometimes, we actually experienced the ailment of the person in our own bodies. This, we found, wasn't the ideal situation. In one instance we directed energy to someone with a stiff neck. Suddenly, several people in the group developed stiff necks! The idea was to send light to the person for their higher self to use in the best possible way—not to try to absorb the ailment through ourselves. We had to learn to release these vicarious ailments and not empathize so deeply with the people we were trying to help.

For the third part of the meditation, the entire group focused on sending energy to each person present, one at a time around the circle. The person being focused on could ask the group for help with a specific problem or request a general attunement for anything that might come up. Weekly then, we each received a spiritual progress report as well as a cheering section for our personal development.

I found this feedback useful both for validating my reality and as an aid for balancing my ego. Since my pride often got in the way of really hearing a suggestion, I needed to make the conscious choice to be open to the "truth" in order to fully receive what was offered me. If I could do this and sift the information through my being, I could objectively feel what was relevant and what wasn't. Some things I liked hearing and some I didn't. Mostly, the group's response to me served as an invaluable, on-going mirror. It was a helpful reality check to see if my perception of myself resembled what others perceived. I investigated the discrepancies and benefited further from the self knowledge I gained

This process helped us develop ourselves as clearer individual channels for receiving more sensitive information. As we focused on "service" rather than trying to prove ourselves right, the information we received went way beyond anything we might personally feel or have a hunch about. We began to understand what was behind some of our personality traits, and this helped strengthen our compassion for ourselves and each other.

Instead of criticizing one of the men in the group for his perpetual and often hurtful sarcasm, we were able to help him see how his fear of being inadequate prompted his habit of discrediting other people. Once he was aware of the vicious circle that made him disliked and then feel even more inadequate and, thus, even more sarcastic and unpopular, he asked for suggestions and the support of the group to form more productive ways of expression and a better self-image.

Much of the objectivity and trust within the group came with mutually focusing on service. As long as helping the world and helping each other were our dominant purposes, the group was a positive, powerful force from which we all could benefit. We each grew personally and felt fulfilled by the results of our service. Unfortunately, it became evident that our friends who originally asked us to lead the group were using us to further their own influence. We were their draw to bring people together. Then, under the guise of spirituality, our friends attempted to control the lifestyle of the group members.

The pianist was especially manipulative. She appeared to be Mother to All—always loving, thoughtful and caring. When I first met her I was impressed by her boundless energy and enthusiasm and wanted to emulate her. But something bothered me about her. Try as I might to love her absolutely, the way everyone else seemed to, I couldn't. Since her behavior and attitude seemed so beneficent and I couldn't find an outer reason for mistrusting her, I decided it must be something in me. Perhaps I was jealous—Bob and her students, mostly male, thought she was wonderful and had nothing but praises for her. I didn't *feel* jealous, however. What I felt was that she wasn't being honest somehow. Since I couldn't pinpoint her dishonesty, I didn't talk about my feelings to anyone, but felt awkward in singing her praises along with everyone else.

Her manipulations were subtle at first. She began by insinuating that certain behaviors were more spiritual than others. She praised the group members who changed their behavior to her liking and lavished affection on them. As she gained ground, she began insisting on specific actions. She demanded everyone practice celibacy, even married couples. She never mentioned these things outright when Bob and I were present, but rather propagandized via telephone or during her lessons with group members. At meditations, people took Bob and me aside and asked how we viewed sex. We couldn't understand why there was so much confusion about our answer until we received several phone calls from group members quoting what we had supposedly said according to our "friends"—the direct opposite of our actual words.

When it became obvious to us that our friends were trying to usurp our authority, we discussed the matter openly with them and attempted to reassert our original purposes for the group. On the surface this seemed to work, and for a short while everything appeared normal and harmonious again. But then we received more phone calls from group members, and the pianist began making inappropriate comments during meditations. She tainted much of the information that was supposedly spiritually chan-neled with a personal slant, using just enough truths to slip the untruths by. Tension in the group became tangible.

Even though it was increasingly difficult for us to attend the meditations, we continued because we felt an obligation to those who trusted us and because we hoped the situation would change. On one night when we had an especially large group, the tension of the power struggle was unbearable for me. Dur-ing the guided part of the meditation, the centering effect of the light temporarily relieved the sadness in my heart. Concentrating on creating the column of light to send to the masters, I suddenly became aware of the presence of two beings, one on either side of me. Gently they lifted me (my spiritual body) out of my seat. Up, up, we went, out of the room, above the houses, away from the earth to the dark emptiness of space.

We traveled effortlessly as if in a shaft of energy. My companions, two glowing shapeless forms, emitted an immense sense of love and wisdom. My initial anxiety was soon overcome by my fascination with what was happening. After traveling what seemed a great distance, I could see a large dark sphere with a glow of light around it. As we came closer there was evidence of great activity on the planet.

We landed and my companions guided me through what appeared to be a very busy city: a complex of many different shaped structures with hundreds of luminous beings apparently in the process of building even more of these structures. The beings, like my escorts, emanated a feeling of great compassion and total harmony with each other. As we visited several different sites with similar building activity, I was "introduced" to other beings who warmly welcomed me. Through thought rather than speech, I was informed this was Jupiter and the beings here worked as one, for the betterment of each individual and for the good of the whole. I was filled with a feeling of complete acknowledgement and acceptance, of being loved unconditionally. Certainly this civilization was my true home, not the disharmonious Earth! At each site, the beings I was introduced to stopped what they were doing and joined the three of us on our tour. When there were eleven

Jupitarians including my two guides, we lifted off once again and traveled through space.

Abruptly, I was conscious once again of the meditation circle and the emotional heaviness of the group. Suddenly, someone exclaimed, "We have visitors!"

"Yes," someone else acknowledged, "eleven beings from Jupiter!"

While a member of the group channeled a message about love and harmony from the Jupitarians, I tried to bring my conflicting emotions under control. The sudden reentry to earthly discord was overwhelming. I wanted to go back to Jupiter's unity. As soon as the meditation ended I whisked Bob out to the car, where I cried uncontrollably. For days my heart ached and I had frequent emotional outbursts. Why couldn't we have the same unconditional love and acceptance here on earth? Why was it so hard for us? My guides let me know my experience on Jupiter would help me clarify my vision for my earthly mission. At the time I didn't feel too thankful. All I experienced was pain.

If the Jupitarians had some influence on the group, it wasn't evident. Our struggle to keep the group as a vehicle for service to the world, not just to two individuals, escalated. Finally, Bob and I agreed we needed to have it out with our friends. We demanded their manipulations end. After an ugly confrontation we parted ways. We let it be known to anyone who wanted to join us that we would hold a weekly meditation at our house. We met on a different night than the other group so that anyone wanting to attend both could. Our "friends" sent spies to our group so that they could punish, by lowering grades or refusing to pass, any of their students who met with us!

This experience of having people use the guise of spirituality to serve their own end left a mark on me. Years later, after observing many similar situations, I realized it was part of the spiritual path to come across such "spiritual blinds." That it was a test of discrimination, to determine the truth from illusion, serving the True master of the higher self rather than the false god of outer power. To see people so readily give up their own power to someone else for the promise of spiritual empowerment was scary. It made me all the more determined to help people trust in themselves and their own inner knowing rather than place their trust, and thus give up their responsibility, to some outer authority.

We encouraged other group members besides ourselves to lead the meditation. This dispersed the leadership throughout the group, decreasing the focus on Bob and myself, and resulted in individuals developing their inner abilities quicker and their trust in themselves as channels. Even though Bob and I continued to provide direction and the primary energy, the group met even when we had to be elsewhere or weren't inclined to attend. It was a common phenomenon when we were absent for someone who never received information before to suddenly be flooded with images and insight. This happened, we reasoned, because any information needed by the group would naturally flow through the most opened channels, Bob and myself. When we weren't there, the flow would go through the next receptive channels. Much as if one wide water pipe were to be replaced by several narrower ones, the same amount of water that went through the larger pipe would then flow divided through the smaller pipes. Gradually, several members emerged as strong leaders and clear channels. They could lead the group and be the main energy for the evening even when Bob and I were present.

Over time, a vital momentum evolved with a stable core of regular participants and a consistent stream of newcomers and guests. As the individuals grew stronger in themselves, the group also developed strength. This was especially evident in our healing work. Although in most cases there was no way of knowing if the improvement in someone's health directly resulted from our efforts or not, there were times when there could be no question that the dramatic improvement could be attributed to the group's work.

In one case a nine-year-old boy requested a healing for a leg that was shorter than the other. He wanted his legs to be the same length, so he would no longer need to wear a corrective shoe. The day before the meditation group met, a doctor's examination revealed the growth of bone spurs on the knee of the defective leg. Surgery would be needed to remove them. While focusing on the boy, the meditation group perceived him as receiving the light well, meaning the boy's higher self was making use of the energy. The next afternoon I received an excited call from the boy's mother. Her son awakened that morning with the pain in his knee gone and his legs the same length! She immediately took him to the doctor to have the phenomenon affirmed. Indeed, not only had the leg normalized, but the bone spurs had also disappeared!

In another instance, the sister of one of our group members had attempted suicide with drugs and alcohol and was in a coma at the hospital. The doctors gave little hope for her recovery, saying that even if she were to regain consciousness there was too much brain damage for her to be anything but a vegetable. The woman from the group requested a healing for her sister and said that she would remain at the hospital while we did the healing so that she could observe the results. As we focused on the sister, we became aware that the sister would die. We also were aware that this would be a great tragedy, that the girl had important work to do in the world. Not seeing anything we could do ourselves to help, we prayed for her to have another chance. We asked for Divine Intervention.

Immediately, a shaft of bright white light engulfed us all. Without a doubt, we knew she had been healed! Not long after, the woman called us from the hospital crying. Her sister had suddenly opened her eyes, looked around and said, "Damn, I'm not dead!"

Amazed, the doctors re-examined her and found absolutely nothing physically wrong with her, not even a small trace of the massive brain damage that earlier tests had revealed. For several days doctors came to review the records and to observe the girl. They had no explanation for the reversal of the brain damage. As the sister adjusted to the fact she was still alive, she realized what a miracle it truly was and became more receptive to life. I went to see her in the hospital and gave her the information we had received in the meditation group about her. We kept in touch for over a year, during which time she had reversed her attitude and was happily working in an occupation she loved.

It was miracles like these, plus the personal growth I witnessed in myself and the other group members, that validated the reality I had glimpsed earlier in my life and had begun to explore with Bob. The meditation group became a laboratory in which I could fully investigate the windows the guides had opened, with the group members as eager associates and fellow researchers. For all of us the weekly meditations were a way of being renewed, of being of service, and of realigning with our inner selves. By the end of each meditation we felt more centered in ourselves and more positive in our outlook than we did at the beginning, and the change showed physically in our faces. Everyone looked radiant and happy. The transcending effect of the light, plus the trust and love of the group, helped each of us to open to new parts of ourselves and to be empowered in our lives.

The growing interest in the meditation group, as well as the more widespread focus on spiritual growth, was just as our guides had predicted a few years before. They told us that the coming time was to be a new age for humanity when individuals would live from their own inner knowing and from their hearts, and when nations would exist in planetary cooperation. Though these things were still many years away, the guides assured us the seeds were presently being planted and that within 10 years the term "New Age" would be a common household expression. It was hard to believe this was possible in 1970 when we could barely find anyone to talk to about what was happening for us. But already, after only three years, we were encouraged by the openness in California and the pockets of people focused on spirituality in the Boston area.

Bob and I networked with these different groups, visiting their meditations and inviting them to ours. From our association with these other groups I realized how truly unique our meditation group was. Each of the other groups espoused a specific doctrine and centered around a teacher, usually Eastern. We, on the other hand, had no set belief system. Our hypothesis of the world changed and evolved as we discovered new realms on the subtler levels and experienced ever new aspects of ourselves. Most of our information came from our inner knowing through meditation or the guides.

With the leaders from other groups, we formed a spiritual council to explore how the combined effort of our groups could be utilized to help the world. Our first focus was our own local area. We convened in a special meeting to discuss what we could do to help eliminate the racial tension that was a mounting problem in Boston. The summer was expected to be hotter than usual, always a precursor to increased racial violence. After much discussion it was decided that the real power we could wield was on the spiritual planes, not in the physical. We would not demonstrate or hold rallies. Instead, each of our groups would meditate in our own way, specifically focusing on creating harmony and peace in Boston. We began in the spring and continued our focus all through one of the hottest summers on record. Although there were various programs initiated by the city and public service groups to help minimize tension, the total effort could not explain the remarkable reduction of racial violence that summer.

Readings

Most of the people I met who were focused on their spiritual growth were seeking enlightenment and the right discipline or path to lead them there. My goal, on the other hand, was to know myself and to express my inner, or spiritual self fully. I wasn't so concerned about doing the "right" thing as I was about why I was doing what I was doing and making sure it was what I really wanted. I constantly analyzed my feelings, emotions, and actions and searched my inner self for their source. In the quest to understand myself I scrutinized the psyches of other people to find bits of myself reflected there. The readings I gave were my best vehicle for this.

In attuning myself to the person I was giving a reading to, I actually became that person for a moment. I could feel their pain, their joy or their frustration as if it were my own. When I viewed specific situations in a person's life, I could also share that experience, but with the objective perspective of the guidance coming through me. I could "see" what actions would be most productive and test the results by projecting into those actions as if they had already been taken. I experienced the results before suggesting these actions to my client.

Attuning to other peoples' realities added to my own life experience. Mentally I "tried on" a situation, imagined taking an action, and then emotionally felt the results. I was affected almost as if I had actually taken the actions myself, and benefited by the knowledge I gained. Even though this experience was on a more physical level than thinking, I still needed to actively apply the knowing I gained to my own life situations in order to grasp their full truth. It's like learning to swim. Someone can tell you how to swim and teach you the strokes while you are standing on land so that you can *think* how to swim and practice the *feel* of the strokes, but until you actually get in the water and put your knowledge to use you don't know how it is to swim. It is still a potential experience, a potential truth.

The actual physical experience makes something "real." It is the physical reality that gives us a truth in our whole beings, at all levels at once. Imagining or thinking something without experiencing it physically is less than the full reality. I still needed to act physically to some degree to get my full truth but not to the same extent that I might have if I hadn't "lived" the experience through someone else first.

In one situation, when I attuned myself to a client and spiritually searched for the cause of her emotional estrangement from her husband, I experienced the whole scenario in myself—her inability to express herself fully to her husband, her bottled up frustration, her depression, and her anger. I recognized her frustration as the same I experienced in my own relationship with Bob, though I hadn't yet progressed to depression or anger. Then, through the guidance that came through me in the reading, I realized that both the other woman's frustration and my own were caused by blocks within ourselves, not by our husbands. When I saw spiritually what actions could remedy the situation and emotionally experienced the outcome—freedom and full expression—something changed within me immediately. I didn't have to to go through the same physical scenario the woman had and her consequential rash behavior, yelling and screaming at her husband, with her resulting emotional distance in the relationship. By experiencing the block within myself, I went beyond the depression, the anger, and the need to lash out. In order to release the block fully, however, I still needed to apply the recommended steps from the reading to my own situation.

In the hour that the reading took, I jumped ahead in my own growth, saving me perhaps years of progressing through the same stages the woman had. As long as I received this benefit from giving readings, I didn't charge a fee for them, seeing the exchange as "equal." I was amazed at how many people came to me with the same life issues I had.

The more readings I did, the more I realized how much our previous experience in other lifetimes affects our perception in this lifetime: how a person who was angry and untrusting in a former life may come into this life with the same unresolved anger and distrust. Although we have little conscious memory of what has gone before, we are not born with a clean slate. We retain the lessons we have learned, the truths we have gained, and also, the unfinished business— the unresolved conflicts. With each new incarnation we inherit a new time span and a different terrain in which to continue our evolution. We pick up from where we left off in previous lifetimes to build on the truths we have acquired.

From this realization I discovered how hard it was, then, to compare one person with another, or to really judge someone's spiritual development. It is impossible to say that a person with a certain background and education in this lifetime should be further along or be achieving more. There is much more to it than that. We also need to know what someone's "karma" is, or what bag of abilities or disabilities, truths or untruths, they have come into this life with.

As I learned to be less judgmental of others, I also became more accepting of myself. I, too, had karma and a history from previous lifetimes that was different from everyone else's. No longer could I compare myself to other people and criticize myself for not being as "good" as they are.

I needed to accept myself the way I was at the moment and not feel I should be further ahead somehow. Although my feelings of inadequacy were deeply ingrained, I consciously chose to stop living in them. When I recognized I felt inferior to someone in a situation, I reminded myself that our experience was different and that there was no reason to put myself down for not measuring up at that moment. Instead, I made note of the quality I admired in the other person and made a choice to become more like them.

People who came for readings frequently asked what their past lives had been. According to the guides, the reason we forget our former experiences is that it would be impossible to focus on the present experience if we remembered everything from the hundreds of lifetimes we've had. We would be very confused! It's hard enough to remember what happened a year ago. Imagine having to remember the events of hundreds (or thousands) of years! Because the present is the most important focus, I attuned to lifetimes that specifically influenced the present one for the person inquiring, instead of reviewing all their previous incarnations. The information recovered from previous experience helped explain recurring behavioral, emotional, and thought patterns, especially in relationships. Marriage partners might find the roots of this lifetime's competition with each other in their sibling rivalry in a former lifetime. Understanding the previous dynamics helped remedy the present situation.

In tuning into former lifetimes, I usually saw little movies playing in my mind, with the person I was doing a reading for as the main actor. If there was a series of lifetimes that came through, the person would have a different (but often a similar) role in each one. Of course, the accuracy of these previous lifetime scenarios couldn't be easily verified. Instead, it was the truths and emotions they evoked, rather than the actual details that were important.

In one particular case, a woman had a problem with her mother-in-law. For years there was an ongoing struggle between them. Often months passed without their speaking to each other, even though they lived in the same duplex. When the woman began focusing on her spiritual growth , she wanted very much to end this conflict with her mother-in-law. She did everything she could to remedy the situation, but her mother-in-law was always angry at her for something and usually irrational about it. Out of frustration and hurt, the woman retaliated, only escalating the problem. It was an unending cycle and had evolved to a point where the two hadn't talked in over a year. In probing the matter, I found the root of the struggle in a previous lifetime in which the two were sisters. The younger sister, the mother-in-law, loved her older sister very much and was very devoted to her. The older sister, my client, never acknowledged this love or caring. The younger sister felt hurt and crushed by her older sister's indifference. In this lifetime, the mother-in-law retained the emotion she carried toward her sister, her daughter-in-law. She loved her sister very much but didn't want to get close to her for fear of rejection and the accompanying hurt. She used anger as a barrier to shield herself from her unconscious conflict.

As soon as I related this to the woman, she started to cry and realized how much she really did love her mother-in-law. Because of all the anger, her love had been submerged. Since they hadn't talked for so long, the woman wasn't sure how to remedy the situation. I suggested that she would have to be the one to break the cycle. The way to do it was to give her mother-in-law what she wanted: love and recognition. "But she won't accept it from me!" the woman said. I assured her that because she had experienced the truth of the matter within herself, she had changed the situation at the inner level for both herself and her mother-in-law. She could now act to bring that truth to a conscious reality. I told her to go up and knock on her mother-in-law's door and without a word, hug her.

"Oh, I could never do that!" she said and admitted she was afraid her mother-in-law would slam the door in her face. I encouraged her to give herself time and take action only when she really wanted to.

The very next day I received a call from the woman. She woke up that morning wanting to end her conflict. She went upstairs to her mother-in-law's door, knocked, and as soon as her mother-in-law answered, she hugged her and told her how much she loved her. The mother-in-law hugged her back and the two cried and cried, hanging onto each other. The cycle was broken. The woman and her mother-in-law became very good friends.

Unresolved emotions and conflicts from previous lifetimes can be held unconsciously in the psyche until the right window or situation forms for them to be played out or released. One Christmas I had a dramatic example of this. As was my tradition, I baked plenty of Christmas cookies and one evening, as I finished up a batch, I began to feel very sad. At first I ignored the emotion, thinking maybe I was just tired. The emotion became more apparent as my heart started to ache. Suddenly, I burst into tears and ran up to our bedroom where Bob was watching television. I ran into his arms and sobbed uncontrollably. When Bob asked what was wrong, I told him I didn't know, that I just felt so sad. As my tears subsided I asked him to tune in to me to see what was wrong. After a moment, he said it seemed to have something to do with Youri.

As he said Youri's name, I started crying all over again. Pictures of my life with Youri in Russia flashed before me. I was baking Christmas cookies in the kitchen and decided to bring some to Youri to sample; carrying a plateful to the next room, I found Youri slumped over dead in his chair. Due to the Christmas season, usually a joyful celebration, I had apparently minimized the expression of my sorrow. Three hundred years later I was releasing my emotion.

Creating

It was my self-delegated job to sort through all the old acculumation of our inherited home. In addition to many wonderful antiques, there were boxes of old papers and pictures, books, old curtains, fabric, dishes, and discarded appliances. It was a dream come true—one gigantic treasure hunt! Anytime I got bored, I went to the basement to sort. Vintage clothing, tools, jewelry, old radios and clocks, knickknacks, silverware and furniture. It was overwhelming.

To hasten my progress and generate extra income, I advertised in the local paper, "Treasures for Sale: come pick though grandmother's basement and make an offer." This brought several antique dealers who sifted through unsorted piles both in the basement and the old adjoining garage, and made offers I accepted without much bargaining. I knew they were getting much more than their money's worth, but I was happy to have help in my sorting. Their enthusiasim gave me an idea: Why not make the garage into a store? I could get rid of everything, make money and meet people all at the same time.

Acting immediately on this thought, I temporarily transferred everything from the garage into the basement. I swept away years of dead spiders and dust and washed every inch of the walls, ceiling and old cement floor. Then I arranged antique dressers, tables and chairs to create the impression of an old Victorian room and spread out pieces of timeworn brocade to protect surfaces and highlight the different items I wanted to display. I hung crocheted doilies and embroidered hand towels on wooden drying racks and filled the shelves with books and knick-knacks. Antique lamps gave the warm effect I wanted, and a vintage victrola playing old 78 records added the final touch.

My "garage sale" was so flooded with buyers the first weekend I continued the sale the following weekend. Encouraged by the response, I opened every weekend from then on, replenishing the merchandise by sorting more piles in the basement. There was no further need to advertise, as a steady stream of collectors kept coming back to inspect the new items I put out weekly. Many left their phone numbers just in case I found something of special interest.

The neighborhood children were my favorite customers. They were especially excited about my enterprise and gradually became my partners. Once they spent their savings and could no longer talk their parents into buying things for them, they scoured their own attics and basements for things to trade with me. Not wanting any new "junk" really, I agreed to let my little friends sell their items on consignment if they would help me man the store. In between customers we had wonderful talks about everything from school to UFO's. Even when the store wasn't open, they stopped by the house after school to chat or show me something new they had discovered in their attics. Their enthusiasm was contagious. When one eight-year-old boy brought me old bottles with porcelain tops by the boxful (there were hundreds of these in his basement) and, then, suddenly stopped bringing them in, I asked him why. He apologetically informed me his father found out how successfully the bottles sold at my store and started selling them himself at the local flea market!

About the same time I finished sorting out the basement, I tired of regularly manning my garage sale. I hadn't, however, worn out my addiction to treasure hunting. On the contrary, my heavy affliction with the "bug," led to rediscovering trashdays. I began making nighttime rounds of nearby neighborhoods with our VW camper, rummaging through curbside trash piles not to furnish the house, like I had in California, but to get my weekly fix of treasure hunting.

When I shared the booty of my pursuits with Mariann, a woman from the meditation group, she was hooked. Since local trash nights coincided with meditation nights, she was a readily assessable "looting" partner. As soon as the meditation ended, we said our quick good-bys to the group, donned our specifically designated overalls and gloves, and grabbed our flashlights. Setting off to fulfill our quest, we sang the special trash-picking ditty we composed, at the top of our lungs.

I drove the camper slowly along the curb while Mariann kept alert for interesting trash. At her signal, I stopped and we quickly jumped out to investigate. Our sixth sense, well attuned from meditation, guided us to the lucrative piles and steered us clear of "just trash." We decided our success in finding real treasure was due to the fact we were "high" on the energy from meditating!

We sold our findings at the flea market Saturdays, and on Sundays I opened my store to sell the surplus. Our satisfied customers never knew the source of our wares. This we kept a guarded trade secret. We did, however, tell our customers that if we didn't have what they wanted, we would find it for them. We took their requests and relied on our intuition to pick the right neighborhoods and the right trash piles to find the items we wanted.

When an antique dealer friend visited from California, he was impressed with the quality of trash I was finding and wanted to try his hand. I had him write a list of the items he wanted and then we set off to wander the streets at random, watching for the items to materialize in the trash piles.

After roving several neighborhoods, I found the things I wanted, but my friend found nothing that interested him. He insisted I had some special power that he lacked. I assured him this wasn't true, but that I did make certain assumptions that most "normal" people didn't. I fully believed that 1) anything is possible; 2) I deserved to have what I wanted and, 3) that it wasn't necessary to work hard in order to get what I wanted. Most people believe what our society teaches—that we are limited by our physical reality (some things are possible and others aren't), that you must do something to be deserving, and that you must earn what you get. Somehow, I never fully bought these fundamental beliefs of our culture.

After speaking of these principles to my friend, he sheepishly admitted that what he put on his list were only the items he thought might be possible to find in the trash. He hadn't listed the things he *really* wanted, because he considered them too valuable for someone to throw out. I suggested he make a new list and that we go hunting again the next morning.

Bright and early we set out once more. Within minutes we came across lucrative looking trash in front of an old house that was being demolished. My friend's eyes lit up as he immediately spotted an item from his new list of heart's desires. As he picked through the pile he exclaimed again and again in amazement. Not only did he find everything on his list, but also a few rare items he had wanted for years and had long ago given up hope of ever finding!

Of course, I didn't consciously review my beliefs each time I went trash picking. I just acted on instinct. Somehow, whenever I specified what I wanted, I arrived at the right place at the right time to find it. When I wasn't trash picking, things I wanted often came to me miraculously from a source I could never have imagined.

When, for example, I wanted some purple slacks, I logically assumed I would need to buy them and searched unsuccessfully in several local stores for the ones I was picturing. Finally, deciding to quit for the day and continue my search when I could go to a shopping mall, I returned home to find a friend I hadn't seen for a while waiting for me. She had just sorted through her old clothes, getting rid of things that didn't fit, and had brought something for me. "Can you use these purple slacks?" she asked as she handed me a pair of pants which were exactly as I had imagined them—and that fit me perfectly!

I observed this process over and over again, but only the frequent comments from other people about my "luck" made me realize that most people had a different experience than I did. That what I took for granted, they saw as abnormal. As a child, my natural perception was of an infinite world. Until I was taught otherwise I had no concept of limitation. There was no reason for things not to be. I accepted whatever came into my life as normal, without question. As I grew up, however, the "authorities"—my parents, my school teachers, the books I read—taught me that there were limitations to our physical existence, that some things were possible and others weren't. Although my mind was exposed to these things, my heart didn't pay attention. If I wanted something, I went after it. I didn't consider whether it was possible or not. I unthinkingly assumed it was.

When other people saw "impossible," or at least improbable, things happen for me, they labeled these occurrences as "abnormal" and called me lucky. I never fully understood what the fuss was about. I accepted the boundlessness of life as being natural.

It was Bob who took a good look at what I did naturally. He saw my manifestation process as mental steps: 1) define what you want the best you can and picture it; 2) know it is yours already (it IS yours already on some level); and 3) consciously choose to have it. Having Bob's definition of the process, I paid more attention to my own experience of it. I found that in addition to automatically going through these mental steps, there was also a feeling process for me. When I truly wanted something, I experienced a connecting inside myself, an automatic "knowing" that what I wanted was "right" for me. Then a twinge in my neck let me know it was so, that what I wanted was mine.

This conscious act of manifestation fascinated me. The experience of intentionally creating what I wanted confirmed for me that everything in the universe was connected. How else could my mental efforts affect what came into physical existence? My experiments in this realm convinced me it wasn't coincidence. The odds of successfully creating exactly what I wanted repeatedly went way beyond the possibilities of random occurrence. I not only brought the material items I wanted into my life, I also consciously affected my environmental circumstances.

When I was lying on the beach one day and a large cloud covered the sun, I waited for the cloud to blow over. When it didn't, I decided to do something about it—there was no sense lying on the beach without the sun. In my mind I pictured a large hole in the cloud with the sun shining through. Holding this image for a moment, I felt a connecting in my heart (I really wanted the sun!) and a twinge at the back of my neck. Suddenly, a hole appeared in the cloud right where I pictured it. The sun continued to peek through the cloud until I was ready to go home.

My experiments with other weather conditions had varying success, but I was especially good at bringing on or stopping rain. At one point, on Bob's request, I imagined rain falling on one side of our car and not the other. To both our amazement, we drove for over a mile with rain on his side of the car but not on mine!

Creating these situations was not just a matter of holding a positive thought as in positive thinking. It was an active process of creative imagination in which energy was set into action through the choices I made. Seeing the results so dramatically made me recognize myself as a creator. This was an entirely new aspect of myself to consider. Being a creator was different than being a capable person. I had always been a very able achiever, most often doing more than was expected in given circumstances. Indeed, I had often gone way beyond the potential other people recognized in a given situation. Being a creator was different. For me it meant that I wasn't limited to existing circumstances. I didn't have to do the best I could within the perimeters presented to me. I could invent new circumstances. I could defy the logic and "rules" I had been taught to live with. I started to feel very powerful.

All my life I learned rules at home, at school, and in a more general sense from the customs of the society of which I was a part, that held my creativity prisoner. At home as a child I was told to be home before dark; not to talk with my mouth full; walk, don't run, up the stairs; be nice to my brother; hang up my clothes; and be in bed by 10 o'clock. In school I was taught the rules of science (what was possible and what wasn't), the rules of punctuation, the rules of geometry. I was asked to: stay on the sidewalk, not pick the flowers, put my trash in the can. Although these rules were meant as helpful guidelines, it was also expected that you follow them, or else! As long as I followed the rules everything would be all right: I was a good girl, a good student, a good person. The pranks and practical jokes I pulled were my way of playfully breaking the rules; a subconscious attempt to change my circumstances and to feel in some way that I was creatively affecting my life.

There was little room to make up new rules, they had already been made for me. Rarely was I encouraged to look outside these boundaries to see other possibilities, or to create anything new. Instead, I was directed to work within what was already known or to follow the pattern of what had already been created. At school I recreated science experiments that had already been explored, solved math problems that already had been solved. In art I was given a pattern to follow and allowed to deviate only in my choice of color and embellishments, then told how "creative" I had been when my project turned out especially nice. In music class and orchestra I sang songs or played pieces someone else composed. I was never encouraged to come up with my own math problem and try to solve it, write my own song or music composition, or take art materials and create something entirely new out of them.

I was so lulled to sleep by the habit of being told what to do and how to do it that I had almost forgotten I was an active participator in life's circumstances, that I could affect the course of events. I didn't have to go along with the program. I could *change* the program. Previously, in college, I had an experience that partially woke me up. I was sitting in a large lecture hall along with several hundred other students. We were about to be shown a film. Some of the lights in the hall were turned off but not in our section. When the film started, everyone around me began mumbling about not being able to see. Even when a chant arose, "The lights, the lights, turn off the lights," no one did anything. When the chant continued, I thought how silly, why doesn't SOMEONE do something! Then it suddenly dawned on me, that *I* was *someone*, why didn't I do something. Very self-consciously I stood up in front of those hundreds of other students, walked up the aisle to the light switch, and turned off the light. Everyone clapped. It was a big moment for me. Shaken, I returned to my seat. Something had changed for me. I felt very powerful—I had made a difference in the situation. I didn't have to wait for someone else to take responsibility for situations and events, I could be the pivotal point. I made a decision that moment to never wait again for someone else to take action. *I* would do it!

Now I was taking responsibility a step further. I was going beyond the obvious perimeters of action and creating something that didn't exist before. My mind was my limit. Whatever I could imagine, I could create. I fused what I had learned about universal energy (light) from meditation with my new knowing about myself as a creator. In order to obtain the results I wanted, I followed the steps of manifestation while intentionally directing energy.

When my friend Sharon and I shared a booth at a crafts fair, business was generally slow for everyone, but I sold enough of the yarn toys and eyeglass pins I had made to cover my share of the booth price and make a little profit. Sharon, on the other hand, hadn't made one sale. She displayed a Christmas tree decorated with little sailboat ornaments she had lovingly made out of walnut shells. Few people had even stopped to look at her boats. She was a good sport about it and tried not to act disappointed but her mood slipped from being very jovial and witty to very quiet and pensive. Finally, I asked her if she wanted to change the situation. "Of course!" she responded immediately.

When I asked her what would make her happy, she said just to have people love her little boats and to sell enough to cover her costs. Then, we closed our eyes and imagined white light surrounding her tree and radiating out of the ornaments. We saw people being drawn to the table, not being able to pass without noticing the boats. I also imagined Sharon's happiness and felt a twinge in my neck. When we opened our eyes we waited behind our table with impish looks on our faces. People looking at my toys suddenly rushed over to Sharon's side of the table. "What darling little boats, why didn't I see them before?" exclaimed one woman. Within fifteen minutes most of the boats were sold. Sharon beamed brightly!

We didn't "will" people to respond in a certain way. Rather we created a situation to which people of their own free choice would be drawn to. I experienced the connecting within myself and the twinge at the back of my neck as internal signals that what I wanted to create was within the balance of the universe, a positive change that would not disrupt the harmonious flow.

On another occasion, when Bob's band was playing in a Boston night club, Bob came over to me at his first break and said, "There is hardly anyone here, can't you DO something?" I knew what he meant. A larger audience would help inspire the band, as well as keep the club's management happy. I closed my eyes and began bringing light into my body. Slowly I pictured myself dissolving into the light and becoming the wind. I blew all over the general vicinity of the club whispering the name of the club to all the people on the streets. Then I pictured the club's billboard radiating white light attracting people by the groves into the club. When I opened my eyes I smiled at Bob up on stage. People began rushing in to find seats at the tables.

Similar techniques, we found, were useful in our healing work. One time Bob and I received a call from a waoman who told us a friend of hers was at that very moment on his way to the operating room to have his foot amputated. She felt that amputating the foot was senseless and wanted us to tune into the situation. After meditating and taking a look spiritually, we agreed with the woman. Even though the doctors were saying the foot was dead, we perceived the opposite. We immediately sent light to the patient, imagining a spot of live skin appearing on the foot to give a signal to the doctors that the foot was still functioning. The woman called a few hours later to inform us the operation was stopped. The doctors had found a patch of healthy skin on the foot!

I began to realize that no matter how hopeless a situation appeared, there was always some way to alter it. There was never a need to feel powerless. I was limited only by own mind, by what I thought was possible. Through the guides and my own experience, I was discovering how much more was possible than even I had ever imagined.

Birth

Bob brought up the idea again of living in New Hampshire. Our dream of having a big house with a large yard and garden, several children, and a community to belong to, had remained strong through our almost four years of marriage. Bob still hoped to teach composition at a college and compose his music. I wanted to write in addition to focusing on family activities. Together we would continue our spiritual work. The prospect of having our dream manifest this time seemed much more realistic with Bob's well-earned professional reputation and our stronger financial situation. We planned a trip to New Hampshire to check out the possibilities. As we drove through the area that especially appealied to us, we imagined how it would be to live there and kept our

eyes open for houses for sale. When we spotted a large white New England house with green shutters and a rolling terraced lawn, we immediately registered:

OUR HOUSE! It was THE house we had always imagined. Bob stopped the car. Certainly, this was our dream come true!

We sat admiring all the details of the house and yard, and then, for fun, projected ourselves into the house to experience our life as if we already lived there. I closed my eyes and felt myself walking through the rooms, imagining myself with children, digging in the garden, participating in the small town activities, waiting for Bob to come home from work.

After a few moments of silence, we opened our eyes and looked at each other. Squinching up our faces we said simultaneously, "How boring!" I was stunned! I couldn't believe how unfulfilling this projected life was. It was dull and meaningless. In a flash, my future with all my dreams and aspirations, my anticipated life with Bob, vanished. I was stripped of all that I had been working towards, what made all my efforts worthwhile. I was devastated. If this wasn't what I wanted, what did I want? What was my marriage to Bob all about?

For days I lay in bed and moped, devoid of any motivation to do anything. When I wasn't sleeping, I cried. All my old questions about existence returned. This time, however, I couldn't deny the reality of my experience. All that had occurred in the last few years, all my guidance and mystical revelations, were real. I had learned to trust my knowings, and I liked where they had led. I could continue to trust them.

I realized My dream life with Bob was my last stand in an old reality. I held it as a beacon to pull me along a strange, often uncomfortable and unnerving journey. As long as I knew my destination, what I was working toward, I could have patience and endure the hardships and the pain. The wonderful life I expected with Bob would be the reward. Divested of this expectation, I no longer had a future to invest in. For a moment, in fact, I had no future at all. I hung on the brink of the unknown. My dream life had vanished so quickly, could I even depend on a life with Bob at all?

Gradually, as I reconstructed a new reality, I recognized that I couldn't depend on a future with Bob, or anyone else for that matter. I could only really depend on a future with myself. It was me I needed to invest in, not "us." Any investment in myself would never be lost. It could only make me stronger and a more individualized, a more valuable, part of any partnership, or co-creation, I entered. Even if the partnership dissolved I wouldn't lose the investment in myself. In my marriage I had defined myself in terms of "us," investing in Bob as much, and even more at times, than myself.

I saw clearly how much energy I had devoted to supporting Bob in his career or into enriching our life together, and how little I had put into nourishing just myself. I did things willingly for Bob, thinking whatever I did for him contributed in the long run to making our life together better. I also assumed Bob would want to do the same for me. When Bob didn't give

equal energy to my projects, I felt gypped. I felt somehow I wasn't getting the full return on my investment.
Now I wasn't sure how much more I wanted to invest until I was certain what the return would be.

The next time Bob asked me to type something
for him, I asked him what he would do for me in exchange. Suddenly butting his head against my change
of attitude, Bob said, "What do you mean? Don't you
see this is important! It's my résumé! My future may
depend on it!"

"Good," I said angrily, "Type it yourself! I have
my own letters to type."

Bob ranted on about how frustrated he was, feeling he wanted something more to happen, something
different. "You don't know how hard it is!" But I did
and told him so.

This triggered a whole different discussion on
different footing. We realized we were in the same
boat, cast into the universal sea, feeling our way
blindly toward some formless destination we felt
pulled by. It was frustrating not to be able to hasten
the journey or to unveil the form of our destination
so we could consciously aid it.

"I'm so restless, I could scream! I want to get
out of the house and do something!"

"Me, too!"

Whatever we chose to do needed to be quick and
without much effort or expenditure. We headed to
K-mart to investigate a sale of inflatable boats.
Quickly deciding on a two-man model, we paid our
$9.95, and headed for a nearby lake. It felt good to

have a goal that could be fulfilled easily and without our dependence on someone or something outside ourselves.

We anticipated lazing out on the lake far from other people, far from our concerns, as we unpacked the bundle of plastic from the K-mart box and used our new foot pump to inflate the three separate air chambers. When our little boat took form we launched it into the water, cheering triumphantly. Then, very carefully easing ourselves into what felt like an oversized balloon, we arranged our crowded legs over each other's to achieve a reasonably comfortable balance. Within minutes we were on our way. With a few strokes of our little plastic paddles we reached the middle of the small lake. Sighing with relief we fully relaxed and dabbled our fingers in the water, momentarily forgetting our frustrations.

"Wouldn't it be funny if the boat sprang a leak," I speculated.

"Ha! Some fun, " Bob answered, " this water is cold!"

One second later I heard a hissing sound. Bob heard it, too. We looked at each other incredulously, then toward the place in the boat where the sound came from. A leak! We stared at each other again, our mouths open in disbelief as the side of the boat collapsed around us. I began to laugh. Bob began to laugh. Suddenly, the whole situation seemed hilarious. We laughed harder and harder, tears rolling down our eyes as we held our stomachs. Soon we were in absolute hysterics and immobilized. Water poured over the fast-disappearing side and we began to sink. Bob slid off the bottom chamber into the water. The cold sobered him up enough to gain some self control, and he pulled what was left of the boat toward shore. I rolled onto my stomach, half clinging to the still inflated bottom chamber and half in the water. Still laughing I kicked my feet half-heartedly until I, too, sobered up and realized it best we get to shore before we were chilled to the bone. We reached shore safely and warmed ourselves in the spring sunshine. Our adventure ended where it began, back at K-mart, this time to return our defunct boat and get our money back.

Our brief diversion helped relieve my inner tension, and helped in a symbolic way to clarify my situation. Bob and I had been married almost four years, and generally we were sailing along just fine. Our dream had suddenly burst, and we could no longer head in the direction we were going. Our relationship had a good foundation that could hold us up, and, if we worked together, we would get where we needed to be. Bob directed the boat from the front while I provided the power by kicking along from behind. This was fine, but I also wanted a boat I could steer myself, a creative focus and direction of my own.

When I related our adventure and my feelings about it to our astrologer friend Gerry, he laughed and said our frustrations were typical of what could be expected with a Saturn return, an astrological situation that affects everyone about every 28 years.

It is a phase in which the planet Saturn returns to the original place in the birth chart, forcing the individual to confront any existing fears, limitations, or karma. Since Saturn rules security and time, its return precipitates the desire to buckle down and get something done, to no longer invest energy in anything that doesn't give an adequate reward.

The Saturn return helps end unproductive paths. It is a time for planning new beginnings, a time when decisions made are profound and provide the groundwork for the future. Gerry informed me that we were already right in the middle of the two to three year phase, and that the degree of difficulty it created depended on how Saturn was aspected in the individual chart. Bob would experience his Saturn return very differently than I would, but generally it created a time of questioning how one fit into the scheme of things. It was often associated with a period of feeling disconnected, restless and/or depressed, depending on the person and the circumstances.

While Bob and I each pondered our future, our friend Maruga called. For a second time, he invited Bob to join a new band he had put together. The four members of the group plus Maruga's new wife came from Detroit to stay with us while the band rehearsed. This gave me a great diversion. I was too involved with the constant activity of the household to focus on myself. As with the quartet in California, this was a cohesive group of musicians focused on spiritual growth. I spent a good deal of my time meditating and seeking advice from the guides for one situation or another. The constant meditating kept me in my "high" place and was a good antidote for my restlessness and frustration.

When I found that one of the musicians was skilled in using Gypsy tarot cards, I asked him for a reading. I hoped he could give me some insight into my future, but I wasn't at all prepared for what came through. The cards indicated that I was soon to meet a man who would be strongly attracted to me. He would come into my life through Bob's work and would help Bob in his career. The truth of the prediction resonated within me and made me worry. Since I couldn't see ahead for Bob and myself, I wasn't sure where our relationship was going. I did know, however, that I loved Bob. I couldn't imagine being attracted to someone else. Without telling Bob what I learned from the cards, I encouraged him to get a reading, also.

When his cards indicated the same situation, I really began to worry. I immediately called Gerry and another astrologer friend and asked each to look at my chart for indications about the near future and the likelihood of someone significant coming into my life. Independently, they each informed me of the identical situation that the cards indicated and agreed to the date that was most likely—a day only a month away!

Since Bob's days and evenings were occupied with the band or with teaching, we liked to spend the mornings together at the beach. Stirred by the nurturing warmth of the sun and the awakening tang of the salt air, a new energy swelled inside my being. I felt very much alive and very sensual, and very loving and affectionate toward Bob. I craved his attention. I wanted to make love constantly, to merge with the whole world in happy communion. Whenever I could, I slipped my swim suit off and swam nude. What I wanted, I realized, was to conceive. It was time to have a baby.

Bob wanted a child, too, but he questioned the timing. He still felt adrift within himself, unclear of his direction, and estranged emotionally. Gerry assured us that according to our astrological charts we would come out of our Saturn returns by our next birthdays, May and June. To have a child at that time would be a great new beginning. After meditating on the idea, Bob agreed the timing seemed right. He couldn't, however, guarantee his emotional support through my pregnancy. My desire to have a child was so strong, I knew I could handle it. We agreed to conceive by the beginning of October.

By the end of July all the band members found their own housing, and Bob and I had our house to ourselves again. The new creative energy I felt made me more restless than before. I had a strong urge to write, but had a hard time sitting down and focusing. I was constantly pulled to the maintaining and upgrading that our old house needed. I told myself I would write each day after I finished the housework, but by late afternoon, or early evening, I was out of the mood or too tired. When I tried a different tactic, to write before I did anything else—to make writing my top priority—my mind always wandered to all the little chores that called (there was no end to what could be done) and I gave in and did them. By the end of the day I felt pent up and frustrated. When I brought my problem to the guides they advised I leave the house for two weeks and write; that the inner urge was to write, but the outer "shoulds" were stronger. I needed to remove myself from the shoulds until I could establish a new pattern of letting the inner, deeper desires rule me.

When I told Bob I needed to get away, he thought I wanted to leave *him* ! With assurances that it was the house, not him, that was a burden to me, I encouraged him to check with the guides. When he did and they acknowledged my need, we agreed I should find a place, not too far away, where I could be alone for two weeks.

When I meditated on where I needed to be, I came up with Nahant, an island off the North Shore of Boston only half an hour away. On the way to Nahant to scout for a room I let the guides pilot the car. I gave over the steering wheel the same way I did the pen in automatic writing. I felt the pull of their energy steer me off the main road, down a side street, to a neighborhood of weathered oceanside houses. I parked the car and got out. There were no hotels in sight, only a man sweeping the sidewalk. I went up to him and asked if he knew of any rooms to rent.

Without another word from me, he physically took me by the shoulders and turned me around. Pointing at a grand old dilapidated house with a long oceanside porch, he directed, "That's what you want." I went up the sagging front stairs and rang the doorbell. A plumpish white-haired woman opened the door and looked down at me. I asked if she rented rooms. Without answering the question, she asked what I wanted. When I explained I needed a quiet place where I could write, she smiled broadly and invited me inside.

The interior was a total surprise. It was charmingly decorated with ropes and parts of antique ships. There were intricate models of various types of sailing vessels displayed around the cozy living room. The woman noticed my amazement and explained that this had been an old rooming house for ship captains. She led me up to the room that was available. It was large and comfortable looking, complete with double bed, small kitchen, and dining table. "How much? " I asked timidly, fearing the worse.

"Twenty-five dollars a week."

"I'll take it!"

I immediately returned to Chelsea, packed my bag and bicycle, assured Bob I'd call him the next day, and happily headed back to Nahant.

Early the next morning I pedaled around the island on my bicycle, orienting myself to my new surroundings. When I came upon the beach, I swam and lay in the sun before finding a grocery store and heading back to my room. After lunch and a cat nap, I called Bob and invited him to join me the next afternoon, to swim and spend the night. I painted with my watercolors, meditated, wrote in my journal, and went to bed early.

The next morning I drank my cup of coffee ceremoniously. Today I would begin writing. I ate a light breakfast and made my way to the porch. Choosing a large comfortable deck chair to sit in, I took a deep breath of fresh salt air, and opened my new writing pad. With my pen poised, I asked myself . . . now, what will I write? I thought and thought. How ridiculous. Here I was, nothing else to do and I couldn't think of a thing to write. I tried a word, crossed it out, wrote another, crossed it out. My mind was suddenly a complete blank. I sat and sat but nothing came. I watched the waves lap against the bank and smiled at the seagull on the porch railing. Still a blank. Maybe if I took a walk something would come.

When Bob arrived that afternoon I explained my predicament. "Aha! The old fear of the blank page, eh? Just write anything. It doesn't have to be profound. Just get yourself going. Write a description of those old pilings over there," he advised.

As soon as Bob was gone the next morning, I tried again. It was a relief to know I didn't have to write something earth shaking. I could just have fun. What did those old pilings remind me of? Old dinosaur bones. The words came flowing out. I wrote all morning. What fun! I felt glorious!

Each morning that week, after spending several hours writing, I rode my bicycle and explored Nahant, stopping here or there to sit awhile or to pick wild plants to fix for dinner. I spent the afternoons at the beach and watched the sunset each evening from the boarding house porch. Wherever I went I took my writing pad with me. I wrote about everything I saw, sometimes as prose, sometimes as short stories. I felt totally fulfilled. This was the life.

The next week I followed the advice of my guides, going home to Chelsea every morning to do my writing there, then returning to Nahant at night. That way it was easy to write in the house without being distracted by the pulling of the housework. I felt detached, separated from the house. By the end of the two weeks, I had established a new pattern of allowing my inner desires to take priority over the outer "shoulds." Once begun, this was a pattern I consciously strove to reinforce in all areas of my life, not just my writing.

Bob spent most of his days rehearsing with the band before their evening performances at a night club on the other side of Boston. The club owner enthusiastically invited his many influential friends to come and hear the band and encouraged their support in various ways. One of these friends was a prominent radio talkshow host, Nick Terry, who Bob adored and listened to every night to soothe his chronic insomnia. I was less enthusiastic about the guy, not caring for the way he constantly belittled other people. He had been a radio host for over twenty years. I felt he was bored and needed to move on. He did, however, have many interesting guests on his show, including many psychics. Bob couldn't wait for Nick to come to the club and had the idea that I should prepare a reading for Nick beforehand and have it all ready to hand to him when I met him. I thought this was a terrible idea, especially so because I was so prejudiced against Nick. Bob insisted. He thought it would be fun to shock Nick with my accuracy. Reluctantly, I agreed, thinking maybe I could be instrumental in helping him change.

The day before Nick was to be at the club, I meditated and asked for guidance that would help with his next steps. What came through indicated that Nick was a very lonely man looking for new meaning in his life. Even though this information seemed to be contradictory to his on-air image and reputation as a womanizer, it made sense. He was hanging on to his position for the security of it, much to the determent of his personal growth.

When I drove to the club the next night, I was extremely nervous. Not only would Nick be there but, also, this was the date my astrologer friends had calculated I would meet the man who would be attracted to me. Thankfully, my mind was primarily preoccupied with thinking about how Nick would react to my reading. It was especially revealing and gave strong advice. Would he find it helpful or would he totally reject it? The information had come through easily and clearly. I was certain it was the truth. I tried to detach from the outcome and focus on having a good time.

Bob brought the owner of the club over to meet me. As he sat down at my table I immediately thought, is this the man I'm supposed to meet? After all, he *was* helping Bob with his career. While we talked, I looked for signs of romantic interest. As far as I could tell, there were none, especially not from me. The owner of the club summoned another male friend, a journalist, over to our table. We shook hands and he took a seat across from me. Now this was more my speed! The club owner got up and left us alone. We ordered drinks and were joined by another friend of mine.

When the band took a break, Bob came to the table, "Nick is here! Come and meet him."

He took me by the hand and led me over to a distinguished, grey-haired man in his mid fifties. Introducing us, he briefly described my psychic abilities. As we shook hands, a sudden spark of blue light flew from my head to Nick's. Startled, I wondered if anyone else had noticed. No one seemed to. I thought I must have imagined it or seen it with my inner eye. Nervously, I handed Nick the reading I had prepared for him. He thanked me and said he would read it with great interest. I shook hands with the other people in his party and then returned to my own table.

When the band played their last set, I noticed that Nick and his companions were getting ready to leave. I went over quickly to say good-by and to tell Nick that if he had any questions about the reading, he could call me. As I wrote my phone number on a napkin, one of Nick's companions warned me not to give it to him—that Nick would call me and *not* about the reading! Oh, no, I thought immediately, Nick *couldn't* be the man the cards had indicated!

Sure enough, bright and early the next morning, Nick called. "You know me better than any of my three wives," he began. "This is all true." He began sobbing. Indeed, even though he always had women in his life, he was lonely and he was bored with his job. "I would leave it if it weren't for the money, " he said. We talked for some time and finally set up a meeting. Bob and I would have lunch with him at the end of the week.

The main focus of our lunch conversation was the band. Nick wanted them to play on his program. We also talked about spiritual things and Bob and I discussed our experiences with guides and meditation. Nick informed us he was a hypnotist. He helped people sleep, lose weight and quit smoking. He also entertained for special occasions. As we talked, I realized how energized I was and how excited I became when Nick agreed to come to our house in a few days to teach us about hypnosis.

As hard as I tried not to, I thought about Nick constantly. There was definitely a strong connection between us that Bob felt, too. In fact, Bob felt that since he couldn't be around much for me himself, a friendship with Nick might be good. I wasn't so sure!

When Nick came to teach us hypnosis, I had to be reassured that under hypnosis I wouldn't do anything against my will. Nick laughed and said I'd be completely aware of the suggestions he made. After our session, Bob excused himself, saying he had to run along to rehearsal. When Nick prepared to leave, also, Bob objected and encouraged him to stay longer with me.

When Nick expressed interest in my recent experience in Nahant, saying he had never been there, I suggested we drive out and I would show him my favorite places along the ocean. We spent a delightful afternoon together, culminating with a delicious lobster dinner. Nick confessed he had been immediately attracted to me when we met at the club and had seen an odd blue light flash between us. What did that mean? I thought it indicated we had known each other from past lives, that we had a strong spiritual connection. This would explain, too, why it was so comfortable for us to be together.

Over several weeks we spent many dinners together, with long walks and talks afterward. The deep bond we felt was strong, but so was the romantic attraction! I began to be conflicted. Bob was so estranged emotionally from me, I wondered if our old closeness would ever return. He even encouraged me to have an affair. I told him I didn't want an affair, I wanted him! Then Nick confessed he was not used to having just a friendship with a woman and didn't know if he could. He began to push for an involvement. I meditated and asked for guidance and gradually became very clear that an involvement would not help me, Bob or Nick. I really wanted Bob and if ever he needed me, it was now. The best way I could help Nick was to be a friend.

One evening Bob called from the club and asked where I had been when he tried to call from rehearsal that afternoon and I wasn't home. It was rare for Bob to call in the afternoon and rarer still to ask my whereabouts, but he was feeling emotional and wondered what was happening. When I told him I had visited Nick's apartment, Bob asked quietly, "Did anything happen?" When I said no, the relief in Bob's voice let me know I made the right decision. Soon after, Nick confessed he couldn't stand having me married to someone else. If I couldn't be with him, he didn't want to see me again.

His decision made me very unhappy. I missed him and his companionship. He continued to see Bob and to give the band whatever publicity he could. It was many months before we spoke to each other again. He called to talk to Bob and I answered the phone. He missed me and said our relationship had been very important to him. He realized none of his wives had ever been friends. He always chose a woman on the basis of having a glamorous and compatible bedmate. If he were to marry again, he wanted a friendship first.

One night in late September I woke up and knew it was time to conceive. I woke Bob up. Within the week, I knew I was pregnant! A week later my mother and father arrived from Wisconsin. It was their first visit since our wedding and I hoped their excitement about having a new grandchild would keep them from sensing Bob's and my emotional estrangement. I was afraid my explanation that it was a phase in our spiritual growth wouldn't keep them from worrying about me or being prejudiced against Bob for neglecting me. I decided to take them camping through New Hampshire and Vermont. The spectacular fall color of the New England woods and the closeness with my parents helped boost my spirits and keep my mind off my physical discomfort.

Not long after we returned to Chelsea, an explosion in a factory caused a raging fire in the industrial part of town. Fanned by high winds, flames spread quickly through antiquated warehouses. Soon the fire engulfed over 15 city blocks with high flames and dark smoke that we could view from our house. According to the news on the radio, inadequate water pressure kept firefighters from preventing the fire from spreading. Stored chemicals in some of the warehouses caused periodic explosions and intensified the flames. Fire companies from all over the Boston area were called in. At first all we could do was gape at the spectacle in the distance, but hot cinders and ashes falling near our house jarred our reality and awakened our sense of vulnerability. Mother began washing dishes, her way of handling stress. "I wish we could do something to help!" she lamented.

She gave me an idea. "Mother, there is something we can do! Come and meditate with me." We sat on the sun porch and closed our eyes. Trying to ignore the continuous wail of fire sirens, we focused on bringing in the white light. I instructed Mother to imagine the light encompassing the area of the fire and containing it where it was. We saw the winds dying down and everyone leaving the fire area safely.

Dad interrupted us saying the radio was broadcasting instructions for anyone in our area to evacuate immediately. We were within the path of the fire. I called Bob at rehearsal on the outskirts of Boston and asked him what he wanted from the house. He was flabbergasted, totally unaware that Chelsea was burning! All he wanted were his music compositions. I grabbed Bob's music, my writings, our financial records, some of my more valuable jewelry (to sell for cash if needed), and our dog and cat, and with Mom and Dad's help packed everything into the car. As we headed for safety at Mom and Dad Fritz's house in Winthrop two towns away, we listened to a news update on the car radio. The winds had suddenly stopped and the fire was no longer spreading. Not long after we arrived in Winthrop the report held that the fire continued to be contained.

Over 300 buildings, one fifth of Chelsea, had burned, but not one person died or was even injured seriously. Our home was safe, and when we returned to it the next day, the phone rang constantly. Friends from all over the Boston area called to make sure we were all right. Several members of the meditation group reported their individual efforts to contain the fire. In fact, when we compared notes, we found we had all meditated and visualized about the same time!

Two months into my pregnancy Bob and I were curious to find out more about the soul who would be our child. We consulted a highly recommended, local psychic to give us an objective peek. Without telling her I was pregnant or asking her anything specific, the psychic told me if I wasn't already pregnant I would be in a short time. We would have a boy who would be very sensitive and creative, an old soul well known to both Bob and myself from other lifetimes, reluctant to come through this lifetime because of the difficulty of the mission he would take on. His hesitancy may cause physical distress for me in the last six weeks of my pregnancy, and I would need to spend much time in bed. The soul was choosing us as parents not only for our previous lifetime connections but also our ability to help in his work. In order that he retain his optimism and innate creativity and wisdom, we would need to pay special attention to the kind of education he received. The guidance from both the psychic and our guides confirmed what the astrologer had told me many years before: ours would be a very sensitive and mystical child.

Around three months I made conscious contact with the baby's soul. Reaching out through meditation, I could feel the familiarity we had with each other and the love between us. I wanted him to know that I would do everything I could to ease his earthly sojourn and prepare him for his work.

Happily, I transformed the spare bedroom into a nursery, choosing shades of lavender, pink, and green for the curtains and paint for the furniture instead of traditional baby pink and blue. I hoped to create a cheerful, welcoming place for the special soul who would occupy it. With great anticipation and joy, Bob and I awaited the physical arrival of this wise, creative and loving being who would be our friend and spiritual colleague, as well as our child. Periodically, we opened the large drawer in the freshly painted bureau to tenderly examine each little T-shirt, romper and sweater we were storing for our son. How odd it was to prepare a wardrobe for a personality we hadn't yet met.

Although I handled the physical part of my pregnancy well, I struggled emotionally. Increasingly I grew more depressed, feeling lonely and isolated. There was no one close with whom to share my fluctuating feelings. The friends I had when I was single had scattered and my family all lived far away. Since our marriage Bob had been my best friend, but he was rarely home these days. When he was around, he was emotionally unavailable and made me feel worse. He wallowed in his own depression, looking for whatever would dilute his suffering, often aiming his frustrations at me with demeaning words and angry ravings. I longed to have his full attention and appreciation, as in the past, and to share this special time with the only person who could truly know what it meant. Instead, I cried for hours after he left the house, feeling like the scum of the earth, fat, ugly and worthless. Craving warmth and comfort, I moved room to room, following the rays of the weak winter sun. In the late afternoons when the house was shaded, I retreated to bed, seeking the unconsciousness of sleep.

I was suspicious, then, when I had a dream about Jack. Since I had not seen or heard from him in three years and had not dreamt about him for almost that long, I was afraid the dream was merely an expression of my loneliness.

I dreamt I went to see Jack and when he asked why I had come after such a long time, I explained that each of us had experienced and grown a great deal, and now there were things we needed to share. On waking, I felt the dream was real, that I had actually contacted Jack.

When I asked the guides about the dream, they emphasized how important it was for me to find Jack and arrange to see him. Not fully trusting myself, I questioned the validity of the message and asked Bob and another spiritual friend to verify the guidance. Both agreed there was some reason I needed to reestablish my contact with Jack.

Even after so long, the pull of the strong inner connection I had with Jack remained. He continued to hold a very big piece of my heart. Truly, he was my soulmate. As best I could understand it from my guidance, this meant that we were two separate beings expressing the same soul. Individually we were evolving on a path simultaneous to the other, lifetime after lifetime, coming back to play different roles with each other, never passing the other very far in growth. Each acted as a support and beacon for the other, egging each other on in spiritual unfoldment. Eventually, we would merge, once again, in evolutionary conclusion.

For sure, Jack played this role for me. He was the one in this lifetime who nudged me into consciousness. I didn't need to be with him physically; just knowing he existed and that he recognized me for who I was gave me strength and confidence. It pulled me forward. I felt we were truly one, in total inner harmony. Jack knew my heart and I his. In contrast, my love for Bob was very different. As we tried to know and understand each other, we had to work for harmony. Because we were alien in some ways to each other, we could learn from our disparity in a way Jack and I couldn't. I loved Bob for who we could be together, for the potential of what we could learn and build. I saw him as a partner for creating something in life. With Jack I wanted only to "be." I was not interested in producing anything with him. His existence made my being more whole.

When Bob and I next visited Darius and Sheena, who had moved from California to Connecticut, I checked the New Haven phone book for Jack's number. There were several listings with the same name and spelling. I picked one, took a deep breath and dialed it. A woman answered. It was Jack's mother. She gave me Jack's new number. He still lived in the area but had moved.

Jack seemed pleased but not surprised by my call. Karen had predicted several months earlier—way before the thought had occurred to me—that I would soon reappear in Jack's life! This was not the same Karen I had met, Jack's wife. This was a different Karen, one he had lived with since they both left their marriages two years earlier. Now they were exploring a spiritual life together while struggling to recover what they had lost emotionally and financially through their divorces. Jack owned a small deli, barely making a living. He agreed to come for a short visit that afternoon and bring Karen.

Nervously, I waited with Bob for them to arrive. I patted my protruding belly and wondered what Jack would think of me in maternity clothes. Would our old feelings be there? Would he and Bob get along? Who was this Karen?

The doorbell rang and there, handsome as ever, was Jack! Karen, I noted immediately, was also very attractive. Jack introduced her and I introduced Bob. We all stood floundering for conversation at first, but soon were laughing and feeling more comfortable. As we chatted, I reached out with my inner being to sense Jack. I felt him doing the same with me. Our inner selves hugged and held hands. Everything would be fine.

Before Jack and Karen left, it was agreed Bob would drop me off at Jack's deli on his way back to Boston. We needed a couple of days to talk and catch up, and then I could take the train home.

Our first evening together was spent answering questions. What had led to Jack's separation from his wife? How were his kids doing? How had he and Karen come together? How had each of us progressed in our spiritual discovery? Karen entered easily into the conversation, telling her part of the story vivaciously. I admired her strength, and felt a soul attunement with her that allowed us to communicate on a deep level.

Jack, like myself, had come to realize that we were soulmates and that we had spent many lifetimes together. He especially remembered a lifetime we had lived together as husband and wife in ancient Atlantis, the same lifetime I had memories of. As we talked, details of the lifetime surfaced. Jack was one of the statesmen who ruled a segment of the continent. Vivid pictures of the large palace-like house we lived in with marble columns in the front, were very real for both of us. Actually, for the three of us. Karen remembered, too! She had been our daughter. Our home overlooked a harbor on the ocean. I could remember the large room to the side where I meditated and focused on my energy work. It was my job to help balance the psychic climate and regulate the weather. I could walk out on the terrace and watch the clouds gather over the water.

I remembered the day I stood out looking at the strange gray-yellow pallor of the overcast sky, wondering what the eerie silence hanging heavily in the air meant. Uneasily, I watched for Jack to return from a meeting with other rulers. I strained to see his boat coming through the harbor. When at last I spotted it coming towards me, I waved, and Jack waved back. Suddenly, the earth started shaking. I struggled to keep my balance as everything shifted. Something hit me on the head.

"That was the marble column," said Jack, also remembering the day. "You were wearing a flowing white gown." He watched helplessly from the water as the heavy column toppled, crushing me underneath. The earthquake stilled and he managed to reach shore. Rushing to me, he held my lifeless body in his arms. This memory and the tombstone incident we experienced many years prior seemed to have a tie, although we weren't sure how.

Although Karen didn't share the memory of this fateful day, she thought she could diagram a floorplan of our home. This suggested an experiment. We separated ourselves into different rooms, then individually attempted to recall the physical details of our Atlantian home. Comparing our drawings, we were amazed at their similarity!

Jack and I spent our last day together at the deli. Without Karen with us, I felt our connection more distinctly. My love for him remained as powerful as ever, but not the emotion. The intensity was gone . . . or was it? I had my guard up, as I sensed Jack did. It would be senseless to rekindle any spark between us. There was nowhere for our relationship to go. I had chosen my path with Bob. Jack was on course with Karen. I avoided prolonged eye contact while we talked easily, but not with the same intimacy as we had in the past. There was no telling what effect those still very beautiful grey-blue eyes might arouse in me. I sensed it would be dangerous to find out. I stared at Jack's profile as he waited on customers, glancing away whenever he looked in my direction. It was somewhat a relief when it came time to join Karen for dinner and nothing extraordinary had happened. No disembodied voices, no floating on the ceiling. My heart and emotions were still intact.

We shared a pleasant meal at a local restaurant. Though we talked easily enough, I sensed a tension between us that wasn't there the night before. I could feel Karen wondering what had passed between us at the deli and knew she couldn't help but feel the strong magnetism and the comfortable familiarity we re-established in our time alone. Outwardly, I kept up my end of the conversation while inwardly trying to grasp the reality of the situation. Here I was, pregnant with one man's child, sitting across from another man—-the man I loved more than anyone else in the world—while the woman he lived with ate calmly between us. I couldn't quite believe it was happening. I had just spent a normal day with my soulmate after not seeing him for over five years! The hum of the other diners around us and the comforting background music assured me it was real. Even more incredible, everything felt okay. Odd, but okay.

Karen stood up and excused herself to go to the restroom. Suddenly alone facing each other, Jack and I quickly looked down at our plates. Simultaneously, Lara's Theme from the movie Doctor Zivago played over the loudspeaker. This was Jack's and my song. Whamo! Our heads jerked up, our eyes collided full force and unguarded. As the past juxtaposed the present, Jacks eyes floated with mine toward the ceiling. I felt myself slowly disengaging from my body . . .

Karen returned to her seat. "Are you ready to go?" she asked. Jack and I nodded in silence still staring at each other. I blinked and came back into my body. My heart beat rapidly and ached.

I stood up and followed Karen out the door.

Jack took me to the train station the next morning. We looked deeply into each other's eyes and hugged. There wasn't much to say. Jack helped me step into the train. "Keep in touch," he said, and handed me something he took from his pocket. "I've been carrying this around with me for years. You need it more than me now. Don't read it until the train starts."

I dropped into the nearest open seat I could find and stared at the small square of folded paper in my hand. It looked vaguely familiar. I watched numbly out the window at the fading figure of Jack standing alone on the platform. Would I ever see him again? The lump in my throat grew very large. It was really all right, I reminded myself. There wasn't a life together this time. I knew that. There was something else I had to do.

I opened the paper and then recognized the writing. It was mine, something I wrote for Jack after he visited me in Philadelphia and I saw him leave on the train:

> Hours before your leaving
> > I hang on and
> > whisper inside—I miss you.
> > We kiss and wave and
> > I watch you go
> My world goes, too.

> Deep, deep into darkness
> > Left without reason
> > or care
> > Suspended with nothing.
> > No light. Just pain and
> > emptiness—and death.

> Then shines the sun and
> > your fullness warms
> > my heart and limbs.
> > Quiet contentment and
> > I live again
> > knowing you will return.

> You must.

Bob continued to be depressed even with his career escalating. He was gaining recognition both as a performer and as a composer. Many of the pieces he wrote in Nyack were played both in Boston and New York by a popular string quartet, and we were honored guests at the concerts and prestigious art openings where his pieces were featured. It was difficult for me to give sympathy and understanding for his inner turmoil when my own needs for nurturing and support from him went unfulfilled.

I recognized more than ever how much of myself I had invested in being a "we" rather than a "me;" that it was my tendency to put more attention on other people than myself. Perhaps giving to others to my own detriment was a reaction to my feelings of inadequacy, a subconscious need to justify my existence. I had learned somewhat of these tendencies at *Farm Journal,* and had learned to change my pattern by thinking of myself first before my employer. Once married, however, my natural tendency was to make myself useful to my husband and to give our life together priority over my personal needs. This role was supported by our society, by our cultural patterns. If I were to follow my inner voice and do truly what my heart dictated, to live from my inside, I had to stop making my decisions based on what I thought I *should* do. I had to stop catering to my husband's needs and desires. This tendency was promoted, I'm sure, by my sensitivities. I was so attuned to Bob, I often stayed a jump ahead by taking care of his needs before he himself recognized their existence.

I realized that the baby growing inside me was my ally. With my pregnancy, I was forced to focus on myself. If I didn't, my health, and thus the baby, would suffer. I fought my impulse to anticipate Bob's needs and accommodate myself to his schedule by thinking in terms of what I specifically wanted. I began making moment to moment decisions based on what contributed to my goals. I knew this was an important step, especially in anticipating the additional responsibilities of a baby. I wanted to be free of my assumed burden of constantly thinking of how to keep Bob happy and how to maintain a smoothly run household.

At the moment, however, I felt overwhelmed. My heart and spirit were laden with emotional ups and downs. Bob seemed indifferent to my needs, and the future with him felt insecure. I soaked in a warm bath and focused on the ebbs and flows of the little pool formed in my enlarged navel when I brought my belly up and down in the water. Up and down. Up and down. What relief it would be to go down, with my head under, and never come up again. Up and down . . . down . . . down.

I remembered the brush with suicide I'd had as a teenager. Then it wasn't premeditated, only a sudden impulse when I felt for sure I flunked my German test and was disheartened at the unresponsiveness of my current heart throb. I stood on the corner of a busy intersection on my way home from school. As a bus approached, I had the overwhelming desire to fling myself in its path. When the bus passed, I nearly fainted with the shock of what I had almost done! Only some stronger, innate urge to live had kept me on the sidewalk. How temporal life is. In a second I could have been dead! In class the next day, I had an "A" on my test, and the boy I had a crush on teased me. I resolved never to commit suicide; it wasn't worth it. If you just hang in a bit longer everything changes.

Up and down. How long would it take for the heaviness in my heart to go away? The guides said it may be two years yet before Bob and I would be on a new track. But then there was the baby. If I killed myself, I would kill him, too. No. I loved him too much. I looked forward to our meeting and wanted to give him this opportunity in life. I also looked forward to the experience of being a mother. Life had been good to me in my thirty years and I had learned too much to throw it all away now. I really did want to stick around to find out how everything turned out, what my destiny was. I was birthing a new part of my being, a more individualized self. A fulfilled, free me. I could wait for that.

Gerry, my psychic astrologer friend, called. He was feeling my pain. Would I like to come to New York for a week? He'd pick me up at the train.

For some reason, I kept forgetting my delivery date was June 24 and consistently told everyone it was June 28. About six weeks before I was to deliver I experienced severe pains in my mid-back. At first I thought it was gas and that it would pass. But as the pain became unbearable I went to bed. Bob wanted to call the doctor immediately but I told him to wait. After several hours of incredible pain, I finally agreed to let Bob take me to the doctor. By the time I reached the clinic, I was barely able to move and my face was green. The doctor took one look at me and announced, "Gall bladder!"

I spent the next couple weeks in bed doing whatever I could to prevent another attack. The doctor worried. If my gall bladder acted up again, he may have to induce labor. He thought my trouble was caused by the baby's position and hoped it would change. He advised me to take it easy, eat non-fat foods and get plenty of rest.

I meditated and "talked" to the baby's soul, assuring him I loved him very much and would be here to aid him in every way. I knew the task he had chosen this lifetime was to help humanity in a very special way and that it would not be easy. When I was feeling better I sat in the sun and read poetry out loud. I hoped the soothing sound of my voice would help calm this wonderful soul I felt such a strong affinity for.

June 24th passed and I was still very much pregnant. The night of June 27th was our meditation night. Feeling very tired, I went to bed early. I could hear Bob greeting the meditators downstairs before I dozed off. An hour later Bob came up to check on me. I complained sharply about the lumps in the mattress cover. After he went back downstairs I felt badly about being such a crab. I felt restless and tossed about the bed. I got up and paced the hall. Why did I have to be pregnant! Maybe I didn't want to have a baby after all. It was all just one big pain.

Suddenly it dawned on me that I was acting very peculiar. I quickly checked the notes I had from our

Lamaze natural birthing class. Sure enough, according to the chart describing the different stages of labor, I was experiencing the first phase: irritable, restless, pacing, doubts about having a child. Now I was excited! I sent Bob a message telepathically to get rid of everyone and come and be with me.

Within minutes he ushered everyone politely out the door and came bounding up the stairs. "What's up?" he asked with his dark brown eyes twinkling.

"I'm in labor!" I said hugging him. We went to bed and waited. In the wee hours of the morning Bob timed my contractions and announced it was time to go to the hospital. By 6:30 A.M. on June 28th, I was holding our newly born baby boy in my arms.

I had always heard that parents received the names of their children intuitively. Bob and I both picked the name "Ivan" for our son. Then, since we had previously named our parakeet "Ivan," we thought maybe it wouldn't be quite right to name our son that, too. Names are important. They hold specific vibrations that affect their bearers. We tried very hard to come up with a name other than Ivan that we both felt good about and that would sound well with "Fritz." Nothing else was right. We kept coming back to "Ivan." So Ivan it was, Ivan Peter Fritz.

In the first week that Ivan occupied his new crib in his own specially furnished nursery, many visitors came to welcome him. Our neighbor John, a woodworker, came several times and said he was making a special gift. Later in the week he presented us with a wooden plaque on which he had carved "IVAN" and a picture of an owl. "Somehow, the lamb or teddy bear I usually make for babies didn't seem right," he explained. "Ivan feels like a wise old owl!"

One of John's friends, a woman whom we didn't know, came to see the baby. I took her to the nursery and let her go in by herself. After quite a long time, the woman came running out, her face white as a sheet. "What's wrong?" I asked her.

"Your baby—your baby *talked* to me!"

"He did? What did he say?"

"He told me about my life!" the woman exclaimed breathlessly as she rushed past me and out of the house.

I smiled and went in to check on my infant son, who peered up at me with his innocent newborn eyes. I had no idea what exactly the woman experienced, whether what she heard was truly uttered in a physical voice or if she perceived it through her inner ear. I didn't even think to question her or the nature of the occurrence. My experience had accustomed me to accept unusual phenomena as being perfectly normal.

I picked up my son and cuddled him in my arms. The woman's experience confirmed for me that Ivan was the old soul I knew him in my heart to be. At just a week into his life, he was already being the mystical child the astrologer, the psychic, and our guides had predicted. The fact that he had just given his first reading, expressing his inherent wisdom as soon as he incarnated, seemed fully appropriate.

Perhaps Ivan was an unusual case, but certainly not the only infant or young child who has been the vehicle for wisdom. Just because we appear young and naive doesn't mean we are. We all contain intrinsic knowing and have access to universal knowledge no matter what our age. Unfortunately, much of our natural ability to access this knowing is suppressed by the conditioning we receive from parents, teachers, and society. We buy into the belief that our elders know more than we do, that the authorities are right, and that there is a limit to what is possible. Certainly it is good to listen to other people who have more experience than we do and to learn from them, but not to the extent of negating our intrinsic knowing. The inner voice needs to be the ultimate authority.

As I gazed down at my son in my arms I made the commitment that I would do whatever I could to foster his independent thinking and creativity and help him have confidence in his own voice. I looked forward to the time when he would be able to share his thoughts with me, the day when his wisdom would contribute to mine.

My mystical son was a confirmation of the potential in all of us. He mirrored for me what I was learning from my own experience: Within each of us exist the resources for expressing our true self. All we need to do is listen and trust.

About the Author

For over 30 years, Ellen Fritz Solart has assisted thousands of individuals to lead lives that are aligned to their true natures. Working nationally and internationally, she coaches individuals, couples and organizations toward achieving their ideals by trusting their inner resources. She works with families, entrepreneurs and organizations to define and successfully attain shared objectives—while helping the individuals involved stay true to themselves in the co-creative process.

Ellen balances her work with people by living alone in a remote canyon in Arizona without a phone or television. With two partners she facilitates several trips annually to commune and swim with wild dolphins. Their work, Dolhume Synergy, takes people away from their busy schedules to reconnect, perhaps in a new way, with themselves and nature.

To contact Ellen: Heartaculture
Institute: 928-442-9262

www.heartaculture.com